ILLUSTRATED TALES OF
JERSEY

PAUL DARROCH

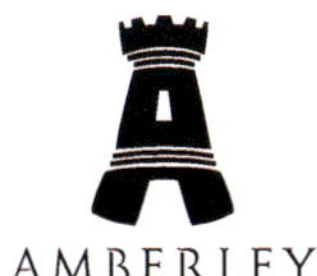

AMBERLEY

Front cover:

The Jersey cow. (Author)
The Tower of Trinity Church. (Author)
The Mary Ann Rogers Memorial in Southampton, England. (BasPhoto/Shutterstock)
Mont Orgueil (Gorey Castle) in St Martin. (Author)
Statue of King George II in Royal Square, St Helier. (Author)
Seymour Tower in the intertidal zone. (Author)

Back cover:

Bouley Bay. (Author)

First published 2025

Amberley Publishing
The Hill, Stroud
Gloucestershire, GL5 4EP

www.amberley-books.com

British Library Cataloguing in Publication Data.
A catalogue record for this book is available from the British Library.

ISBN 978 1 3981 2389 2 (paperback)
ISBN 978 1 3981 2390 8 (ebook)

Origination by Amberley Publishing.
Printed in Great Britain.

Appointed GPSR EU Representative:
Easy Access System Europe Oü, 16879218
Address: Mustamäe tee 50, 10621, Tallinn, Estonia
Contact Details: gpsr.requests@easproject.com, +358 40 500 3575

Contents

Introduction 5

The Dragon of Jersey 11

Tales of the West 18

   The Lost Manor of La Brecquette 23

   De Carteret's Leap 28

   Janvrin's Tomb 33

Tales of the North Coast 37

   Les Cris des Tombelènes: A Medieval Tragedy 40

   The Storm Hound of Bouley 45

Tales of Town 50

   The Sails of Saint Helier 52

   The Lost Stones of Jersey 58

   The Doomed Ship: A Channel Tragedy 62

Tales of the East 68

   The Lost Bridge to France 71

   The Bull of St Clement 77

   The Hermit King 82

   Geoffrey's Leap 90

Postscript 95

Acknowledgements 96

About the Author 96

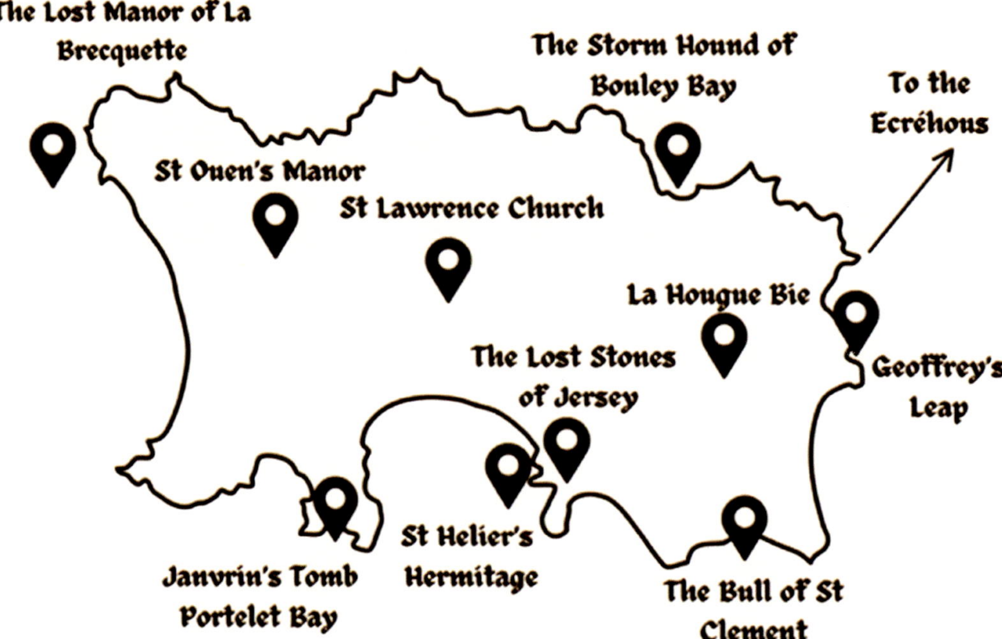

Map of the Island of Jersey. (Paul Darroch, based on a vector file from EllenVD/ Shutterstock.com)

Introduction

Thousands of miles of clear cold ocean lie between St Ouen's Bay and the nearest westerly shore. In ancient times, Jersey seemed to be poised on the edge of eternity, an island shrouded in fog, peppered with mysterious dolmens.

Jersey might be a mere 9 miles by 5, doubling in size with its lowest tide; yet it is rich in ancient tales, handed down through the generations in its native tongue of Jèrriais. The terrifying power of the sea, as a force of mutability and destruction, lies behind so many of Jersey's ancient myths.

A modern traveller might assume that the splendid coastline, its stark granite cliffs and sandy beaches, must be as old as the hills. Yet our precious shores are barely a few thousand years young, carved out in the blink of a geological eye.

We are perched here above the flood. All around us lies the original, drowned world; the hunting trails of our ancestors that have been swept away by the waves. Around six or seven thousand years ago, the land bridge to the continent was finally severed. The Island of Jersey was born.

Folk memories of an older world lingered on. Consider the curious legend of La Planche, featuring a sixth-century bishop who crossed a wooden bridge from

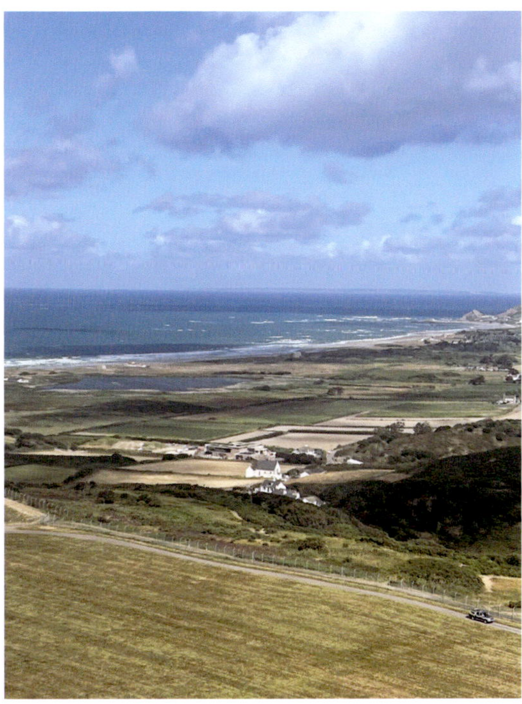

St Ouen's Bay. (Author)

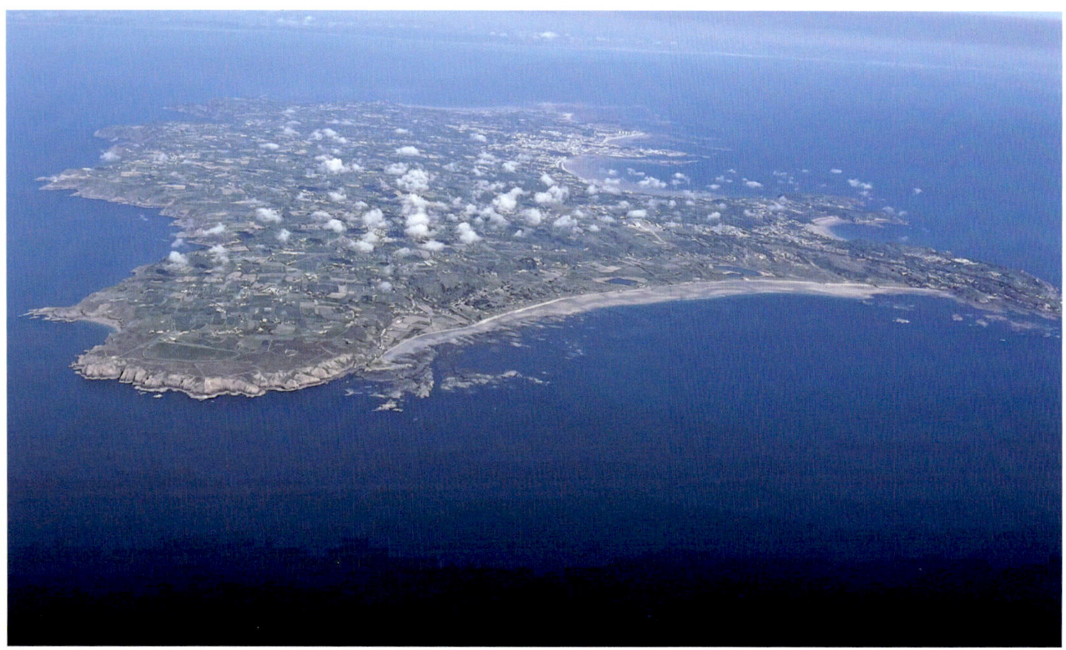

Aerial view of Jersey. (Author)

Normandy to the Ecréhous reef, which lies to the north-east of Jersey. Another local myth tells of the lost manor of La Brecquette, which nestled amid rich orchards in St Ouen. Legend says that on one terrible night in 1356, it was swept away in a violent tempest: simply erased from the map.

The churning seas brought successive waves of terror: raiding parties, smugglers, ferocious storms, and the fear of the rising tide. Many of the ancient legends recounted in this book – of the Bull of St Clement, the Cris des Tombelènes and the Black Dog of Bouley Bay – give voice to these ancient, lingering fears. In the wake of the fall of the Roman Empire, the world seemed chaotic and frightening. The land and sea were teeming with mystery. Stories were one way to bring sense to a terrifying world.

Eventually William the Conqueror, Duke of Normandy, seized the English throne. The Channel Islands became the only surviving remnant of his ancient domain. Perched on the frontier of clashing kingdoms, the Island would spin new legends. Stories are one way that a culture reveals itself, and how voices from centuries past continue to speak to us today.

In these pages you will discover many of Jersey's most famous tales. We will travel from the western parishes to the desolate cliffs of the north coast, to the thriving capital of St Helier, and finally to the tranquil east, where France sometimes seems close enough to touch.

We begin with one of the oldest legends of them all, of the fearsome dragon that once tormented Jersey, unbound and seething, and whose breath was pure fire.

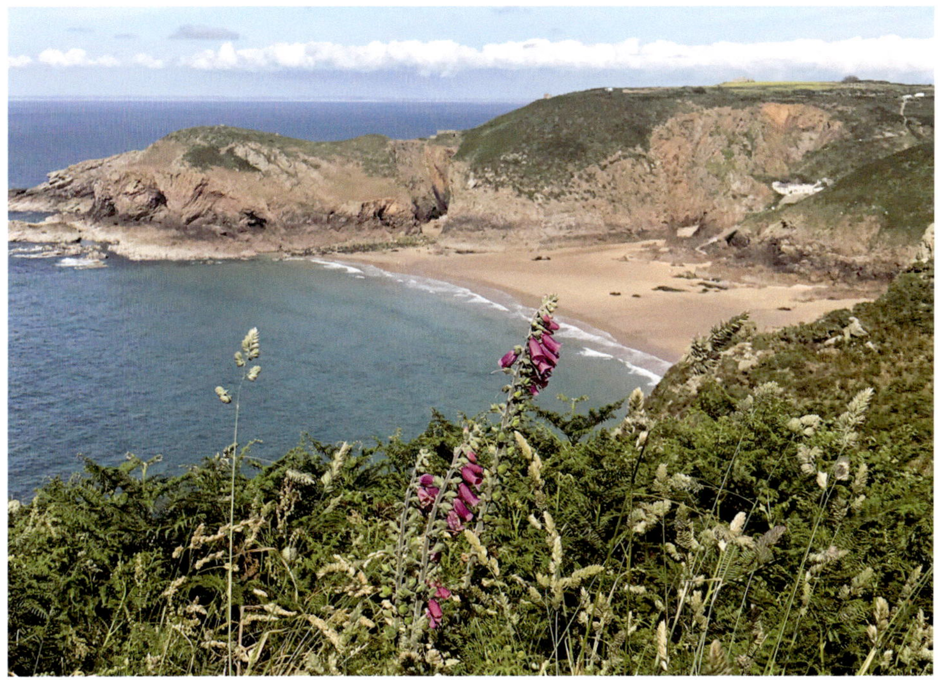

A glimpse of Plémont. (Author)

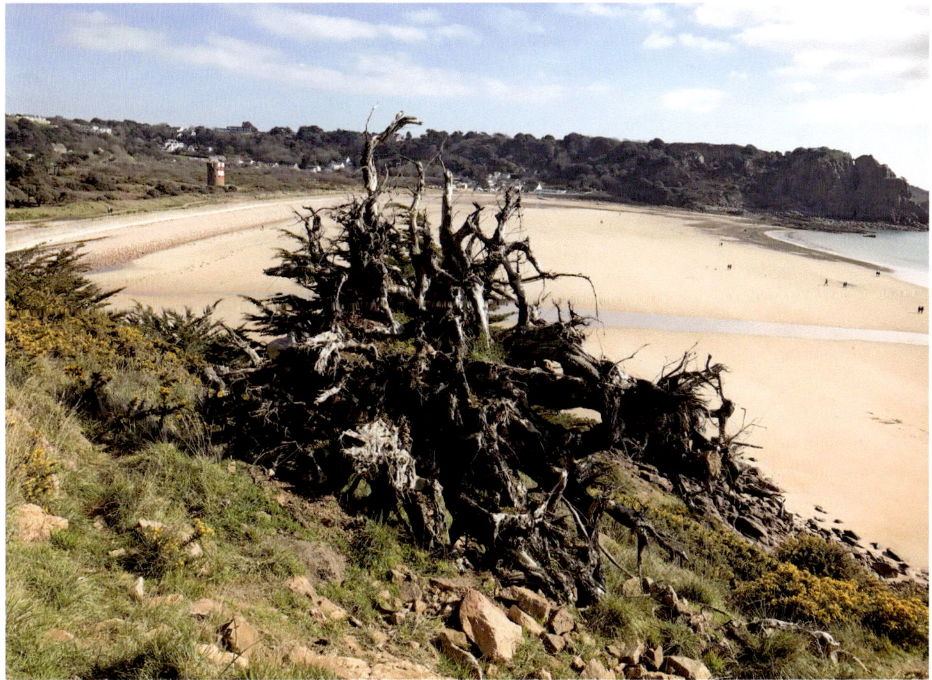

A view of Ouaisné. (Author)

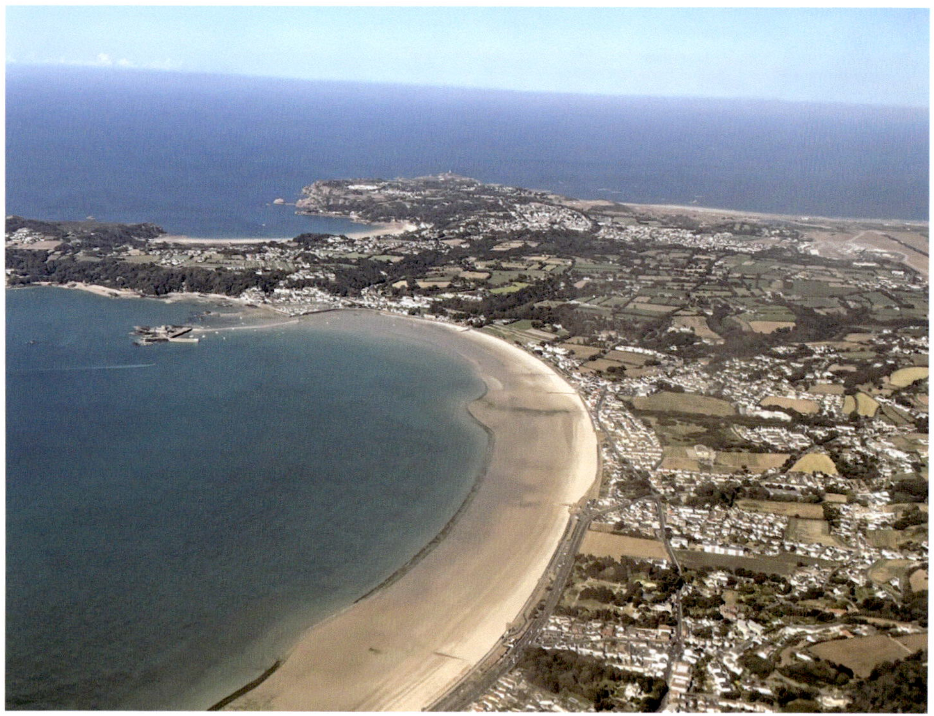

Aerial view of south-western Jersey. (Author)

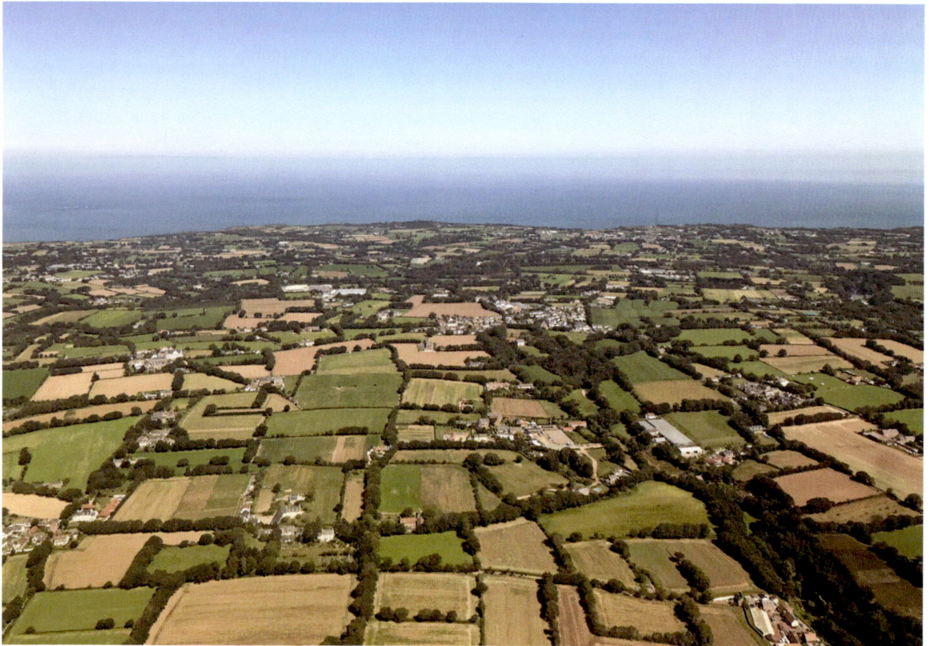

Fields in the northern parishes. (Author)

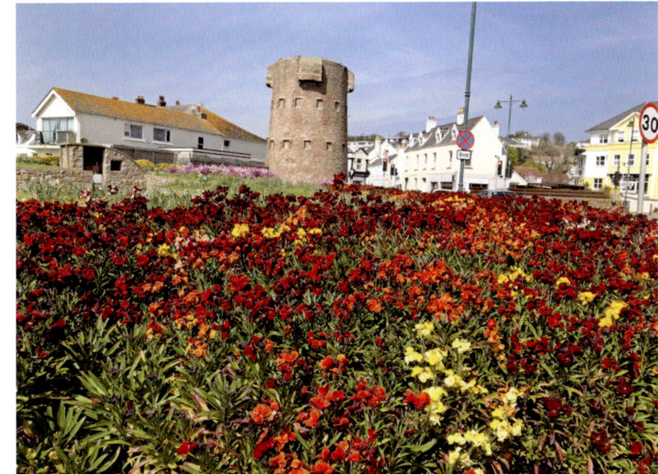

Flowers at First Tower. (Author)

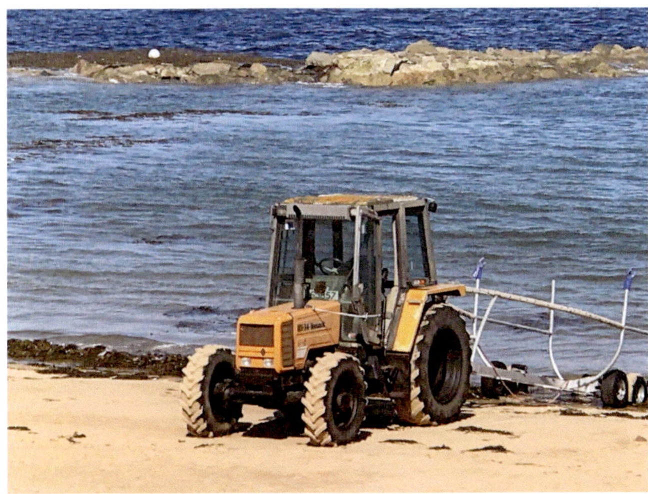

Harvesting *vraic* (seaweed) at Grève de Lecq. (Author)

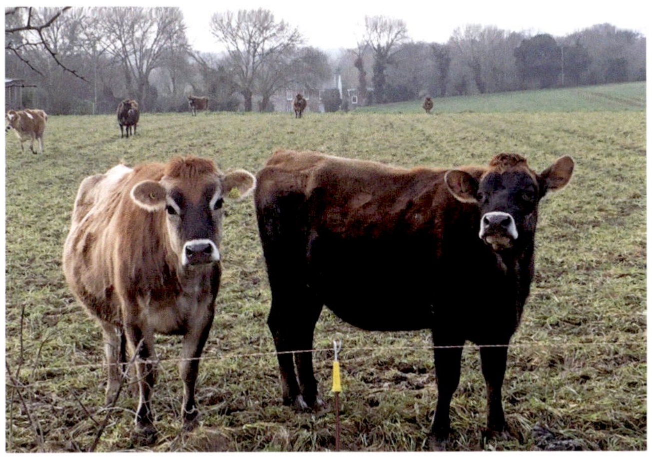

Jersey cows in winter. (Author)

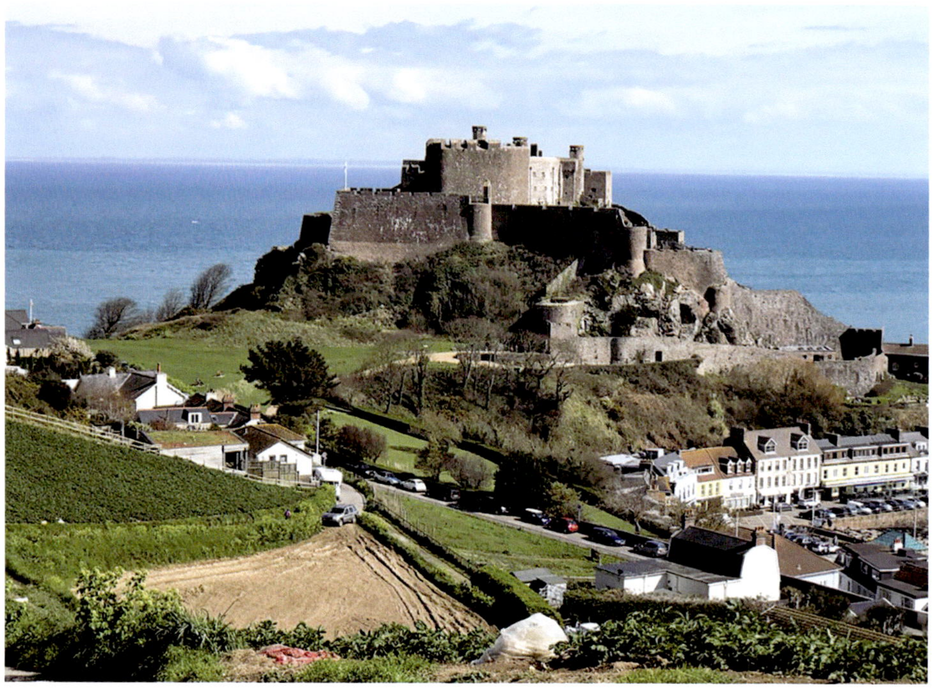

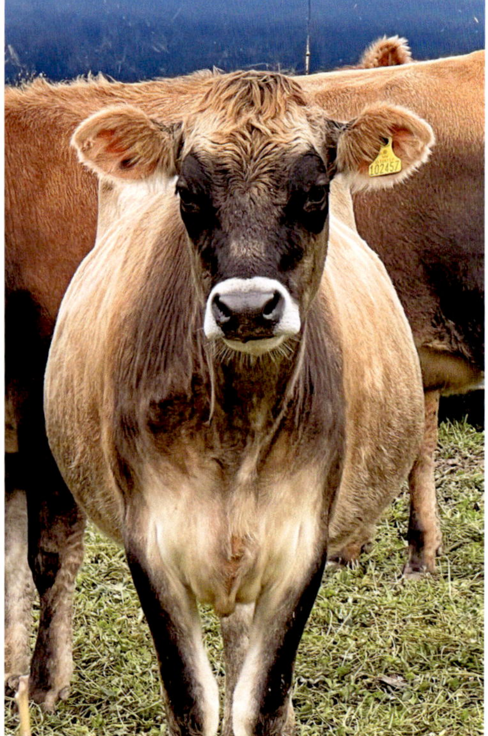

Above: Mont Orgueil, or Gorey Castle, in St Martin. (Author)

Left: The Jersey cow. (Author)

The Dragon of Jersey

This story is based on a medieval legend. It probably dates from the twelfth century and reflects the close relationship between Jersey and the mainland of Normandy.

The Channel Islands, they whispered, were stepping-stones, forming a bridge between earth and heaven. They lay to the west of the Norman peninsula, in the arms of the setting sun; steps in a celestial ladder that reached to the skies.

The greatest of them all was Jersey. Latticed by dolmens, barely touched by Roman hands, it remained a hooded and mysterious realm. Sea and land were woven together here. At low tide, the seabed dried to reveal a mosaic of rocks and silent pools. This sandy kingdom would drown as the hourglass emptied, swamped by the flood tide.

The dragon that ruled the island slept by the shores of St Lawrence, where the tides poured in across the bay and collided with the dunes. This was deep and treacherous bogland, a maze of marram grass. Green marsh-fires burned here night and day, ghostly flames dancing over the sands. On moonless nights such as these, the dread beast would stir.

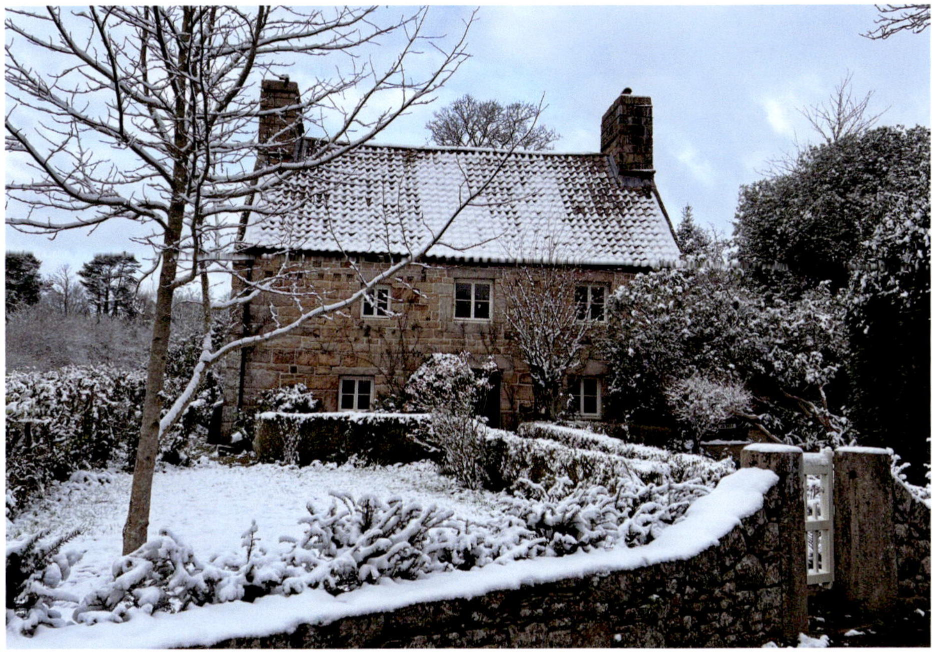

Le Rât Cottage in the snow. (Author)

The dragon crept inside their dreams at first, tormenting the peasant on her straw mat, the fat Seigneur between his ermine sheets. Each sleeper first heard the rhythmic beating of scaly, bony wings, echoing through the chambers of the night. Each dreamer glimpsed its emerald scales, its savage lantern eyes. Sometimes it swooped down like a falcon, lunging at their children, ravaging their precious crops. Sometimes its lightning breath tore up the sky, setting the woods ablaze, exulting when homesteads burned.

Desperate families fled to the stone sanctuary of St Lawrence's Church, barricading the doors, prostrating themselves before the altar until the terror overhead had passed. On brighter days, they tried to forget their creeping fear, pretended it but was a winter's tale, until the teeth-marks in the barns, and the scorched orchards put the lie to their denials.

The dragon was growing stronger, fed by fear. It began to devour a greater portion of the land and razed entire cornfields with its fiery breath. So, the villagers of St Lawrence called for their Rector, a holy man who knew the secret lore of letters. He penned an urgent plea, in clunky Latin, to the distant Seigneur of Hambie in Normandy. They said he was the bravest and strongest knight who lived across the sea, and so they begged him for rescue.

Their prayers were answered. In those days, the rickety 'planche' or wooden bridge from Normandy to the Ecréhous reef near Jersey was still standing. The Seigneur boldly marched over the waters, his squire at his side. He was advancing

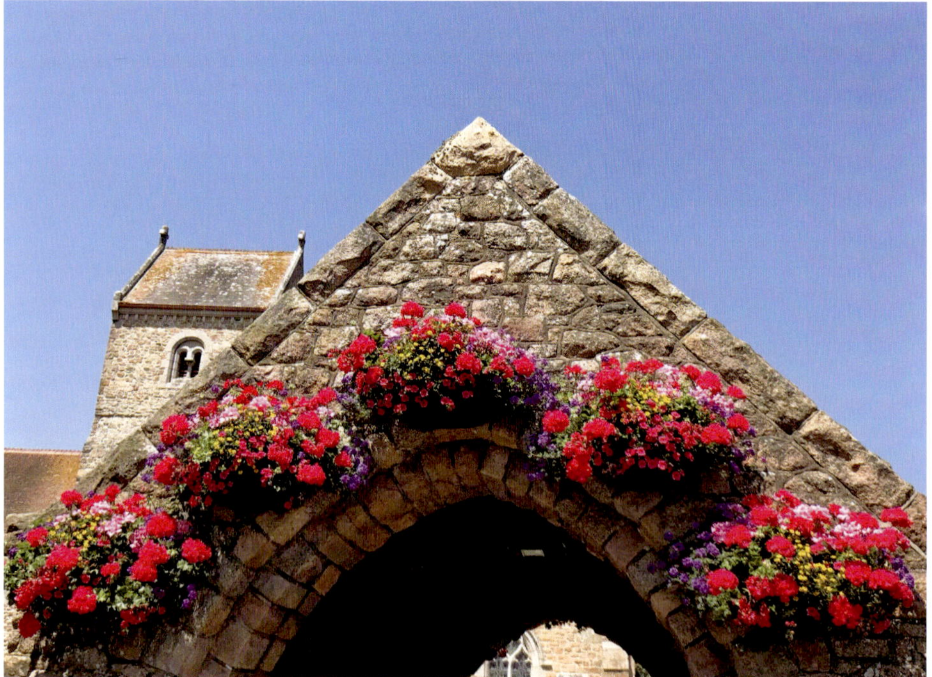

Floral arch at St Lawrence Parish Church. (Author)

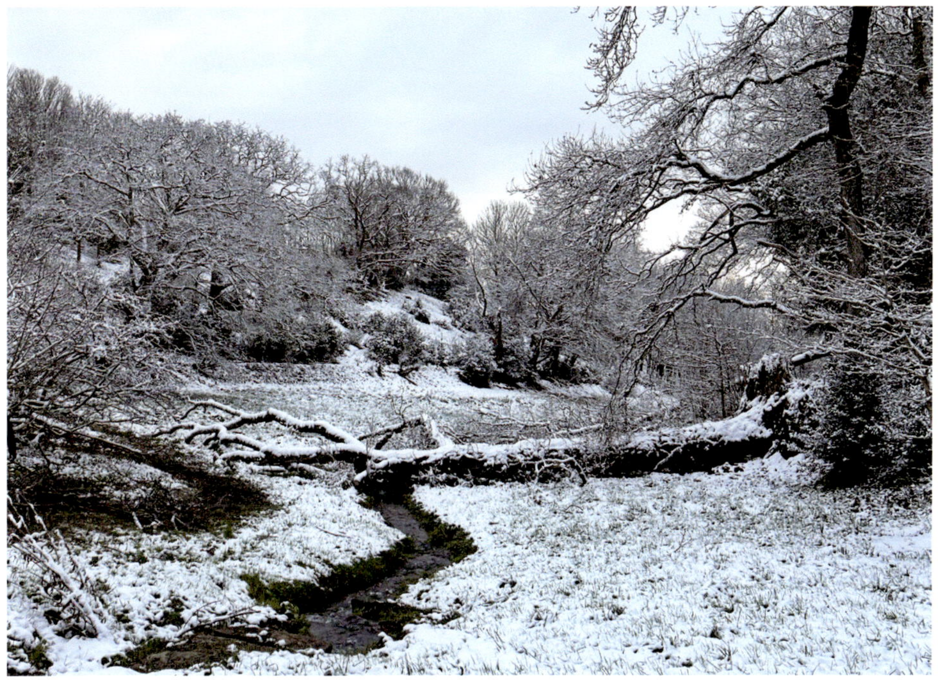

St Lawrence countryside in snow. (Author)

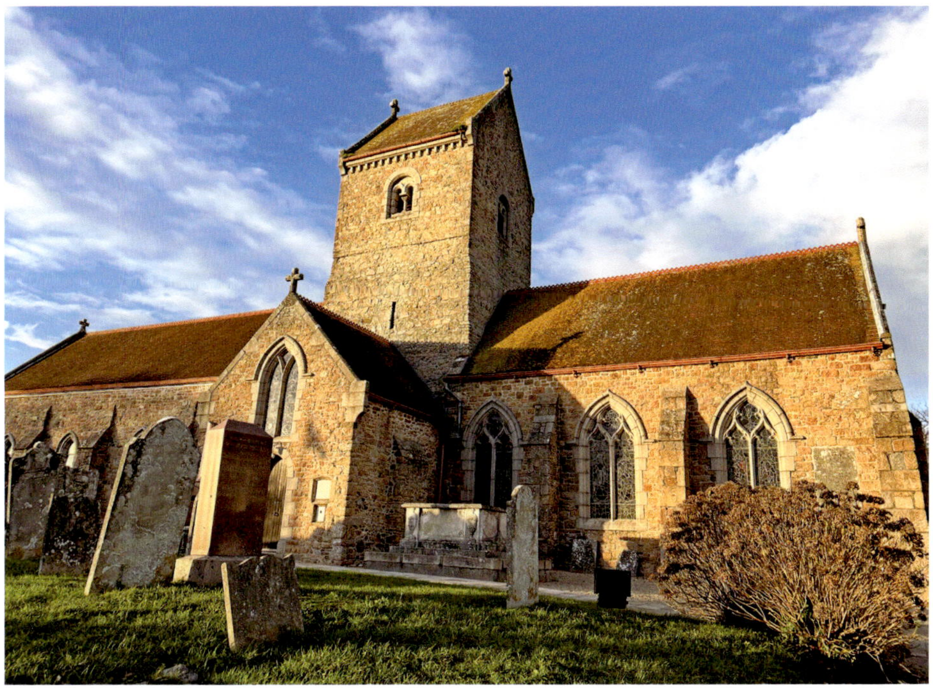

St Lawrence Parish Church. (Author)

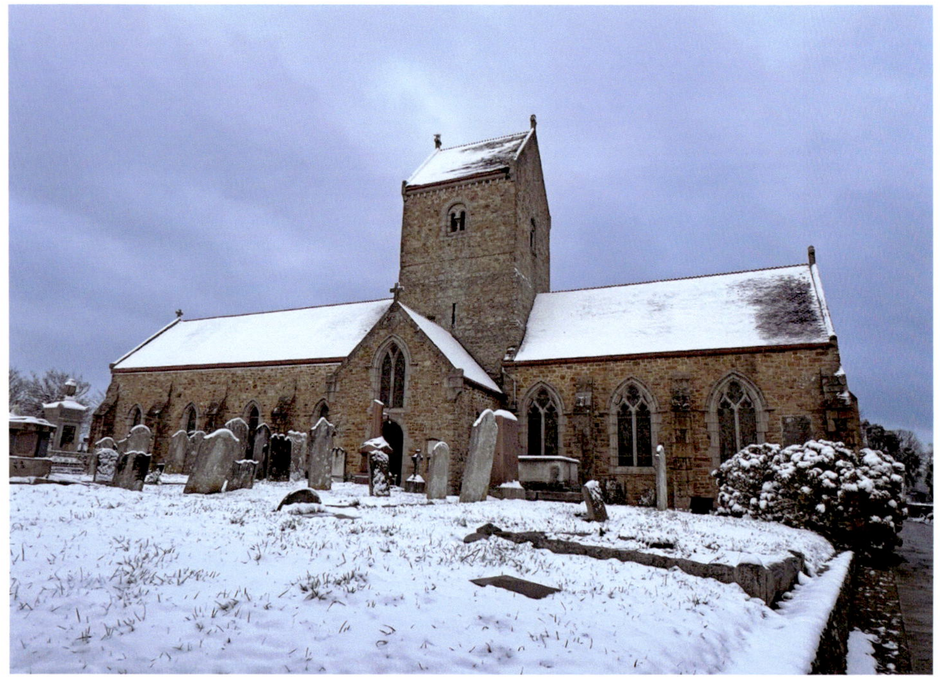

St Lawrence Parish Church in the snow. (Author)

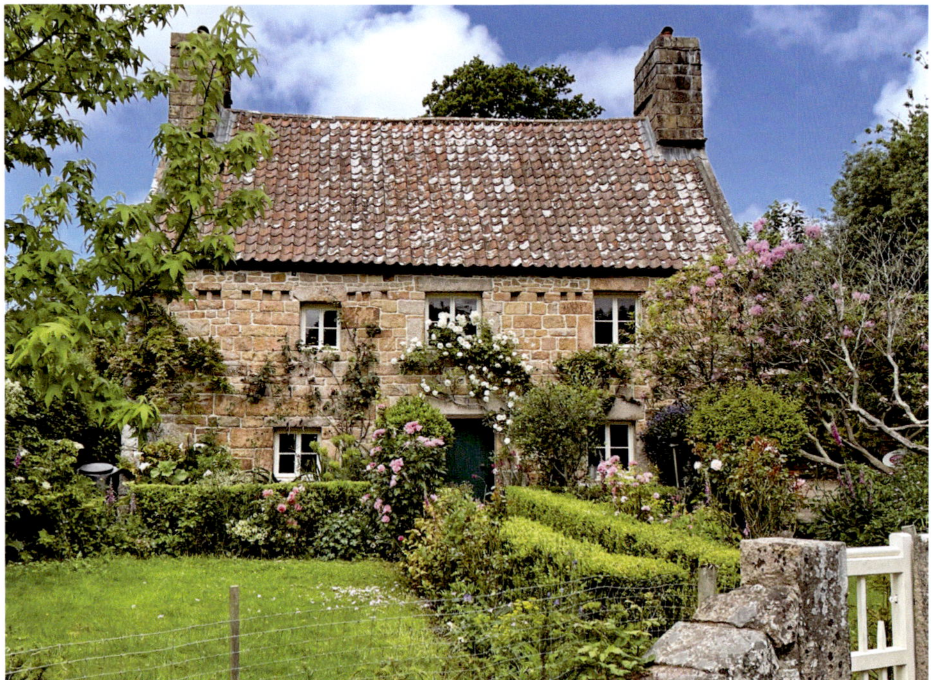

Le Rât Cottage in St Lawrence. (Author)

in years now, his black hair flecked with silver, a wounded veteran scarred by decades of struggle. Still, his faith and fight were both undimmed. He bore the Chi Rho emblem of the Emperor Constantine on his shield, and two burnished leopards on his banner. His squire, Hugo, was a strapping lad of eighteen, with the raw energy of a hunting dog, but eyes as grey as granite. At the Ecréhous reef, they faced a deep channel of water. A barque with torches carried them west, until eventually they landed at the long beach of Grouville. The dragon wheeled in the sky above, watching the travellers, waiting for the struggle it knew was coming soon.

Summer breathed its warmth upon Jersey. For a month, Sir Hambie and his squire lived on the land, brothers-in-arms on a noble quest, tracking down their sworn foe. They finally stumbled across the dragon on the longest day of the year, when the sun streamed over the horizon and hung like a red copper plate in the sky. Their clash of steel rang out for hours like a blacksmith's anvil; the battle between honest blade and raging claw. The Seigneur sliced the tail off the great worm, but it roared in vengeance and set the lord on fire. The foul marsh-water extinguished the flame, but the Seigneur was charred and wounded.

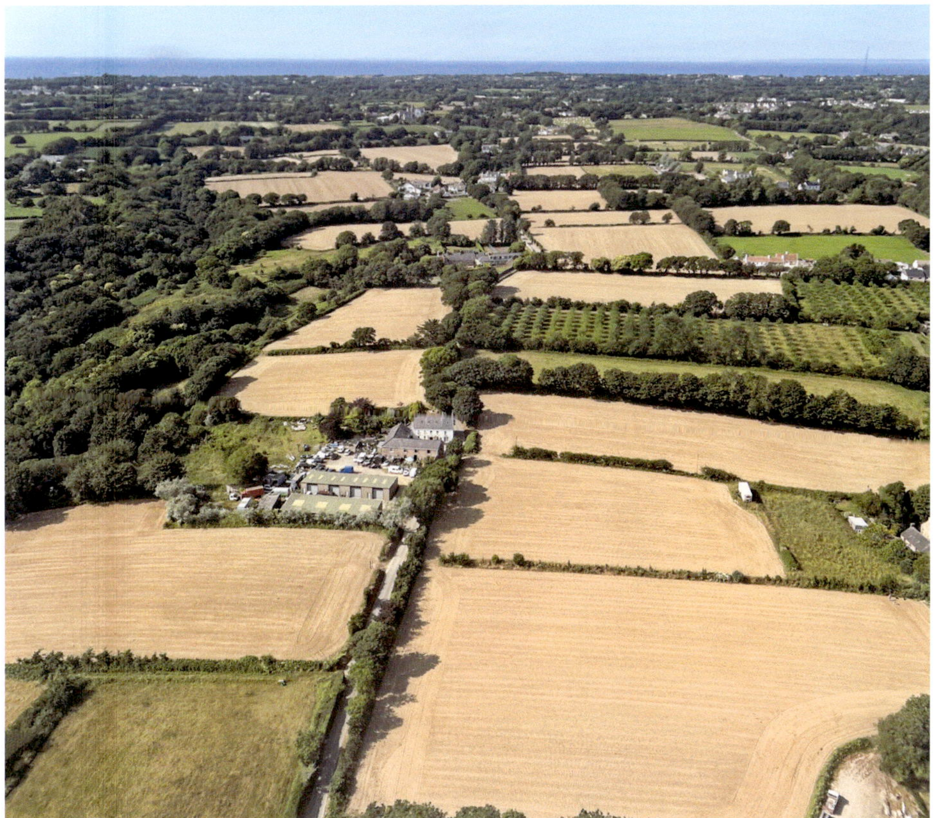

The Jersey countryside. (Author)

As the heat of noonday burst forth, the tables turned at last. The dragon drew its strength from shade and dark, and as they duelled in blazing sunshine its ferocity waned, and its strength withered. At the third hour, with a final cry, the Seigneur raised his golden sword to the sky and slashed the dragon's brain clean through. The serpent coiled in agony, then went limp. Its scales sheared off one by one like tears, and it sank back into the mud. The foul dragon of St Lawrence had been slain.

Sir Hambie lay burned and bruised, and blood flowed from his side. He staggered as if to drink fresh wine, as the marshland span around him. He beckoned for his loyal squire to tend his wounds. Hugo sauntered over, but instead of succour he brandished a hunting knife. Sir Hambie was too weak to fight him. His throat was slashed, a spreading red ribbon, and he bled to death in the fetid marsh.

Hugo returned to his master's castle in Normandy, robed in his stolen glory. When he arrived at the gates of Hambie, the Lady of the Castle begged for news of her beloved husband. His tearful story had the beguiling illusion of truth. 'Your husband died a hero. The dragon slew him, but in righteous anger I rose up myself and killed the beast.' The beautiful, broken widow was touched to the core, so Hugo weaved his final and most insidious lie. 'His very last wish, my Lady, was that I might prove myself worthy of your love.'

He cajoled and caressed her in her grief, and before long he wed the Lady. The grand fountains and estates of Hambie, the four-poster bed, and the blind devotion of a grieving wife had fallen into his lap like stolen treasure. The circle of deception was complete. Then one day the dragon, its scales shimmering in moon-fire, returned. Beating wings started to haunt his dreams.

Midnight at the lord's castle. A screeching cry, a slashing tail – and the dragon's eye fixed the pretender with a hypnotic grip. Hugo was compelled by his nightmare to scream out the truth. 'I killed him! I killed the Seigneur of Hambie! I declare my crime!' The Lady nestling in his arms was woken by the scream of his confession. Suddenly the cold ring of truth clattered like a dagger dropped on flagstones. She summoned her guardsman to question this cuckoo in her bed. Under interrogation, he confessed his crime.

The Lady of Hambie was merciless in her rage. Hugo was hung from the highest tree, and his corpse was thrown to the dogs. She had been seduced by his lies; now she would see that her noble first husband's memory was honoured for ever.

So, she travelled to that far country, to the island of mists and treasure, where the marsh-fires still burned on the shores of the bay. The people of Jersey remembered the brave knight who had come this way and had rid them of the terrible beast. They had safeguarded his body in a stone chamber, and it showed no sign of decay. So, she carried his miraculously preserved body to a holy and beautiful place in the east of the Isle and raised a hill of earth to mark his passing.

The great mound stood proud and tall, a gigantic grave-marker that she could glimpse even from her château in Normandy. She dubbed it *La Hougue de Hambie*; later generations would truncate the name to *La Hougue Bie*.

The wheel of history turned, and the old world changed. In time the marshes of fire were drained, the bridge to the Ecréhous sank, and the age of dragons fell into legend. Later, they would build a stone chapel on the summit, the better to remember their hero's name. They say the Seigneur of Hambie sleeps there still, buried by the fallen centuries, his sword by his side. The seasons turn, and time empties its hourglass, and he watches us silently from beneath his carpet of grass and leaves.

They say the dragon did not entirely vanish either. His fire was gone, but his shadow remained. He found his way through to other realms, other dreams.

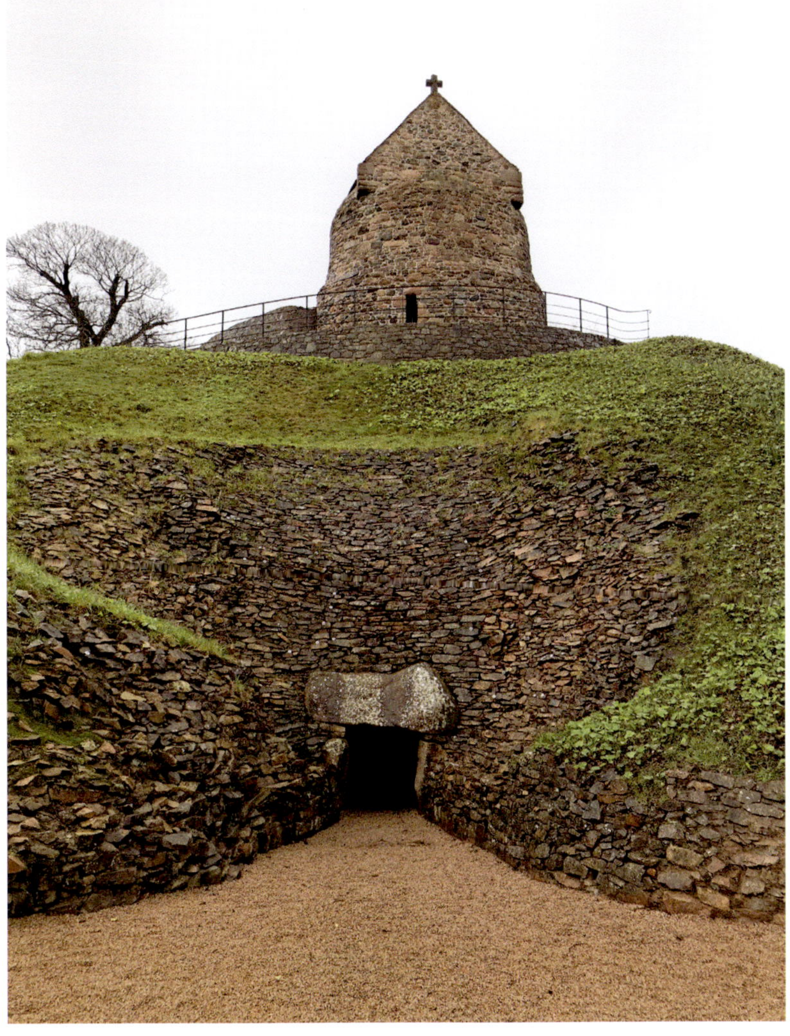

La Hougue Bie.
(Author)

Tales of the West

Let us turn west, towards a landscape defined by the great crescent of St Ouen's Bay. From the rocks at Corbière to the headland at l'Etacq and the broken castle at Grosnez beyond, the western landscape is rich in myth and mystery. The power of the ocean is palpable here: destructive, capricious and unyielding. Our first legend from the west, a late medieval tale, speaks of its violent energy.

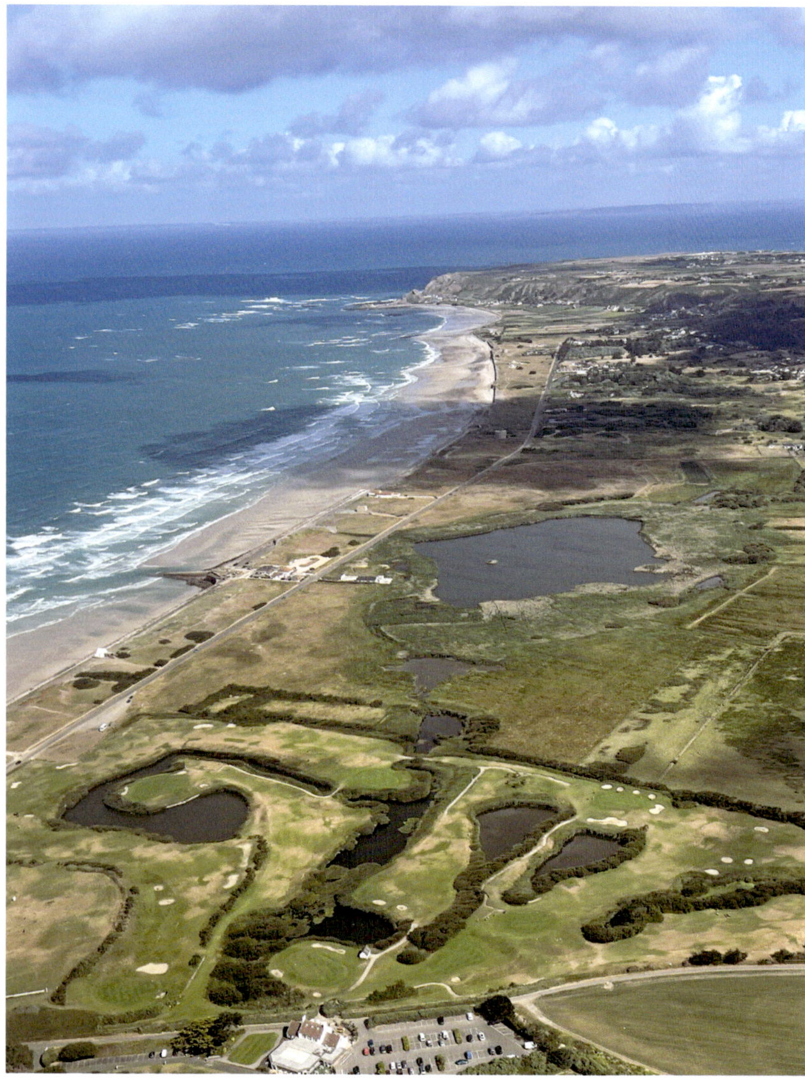

Aerial view of St Ouen's Bay. (Author)

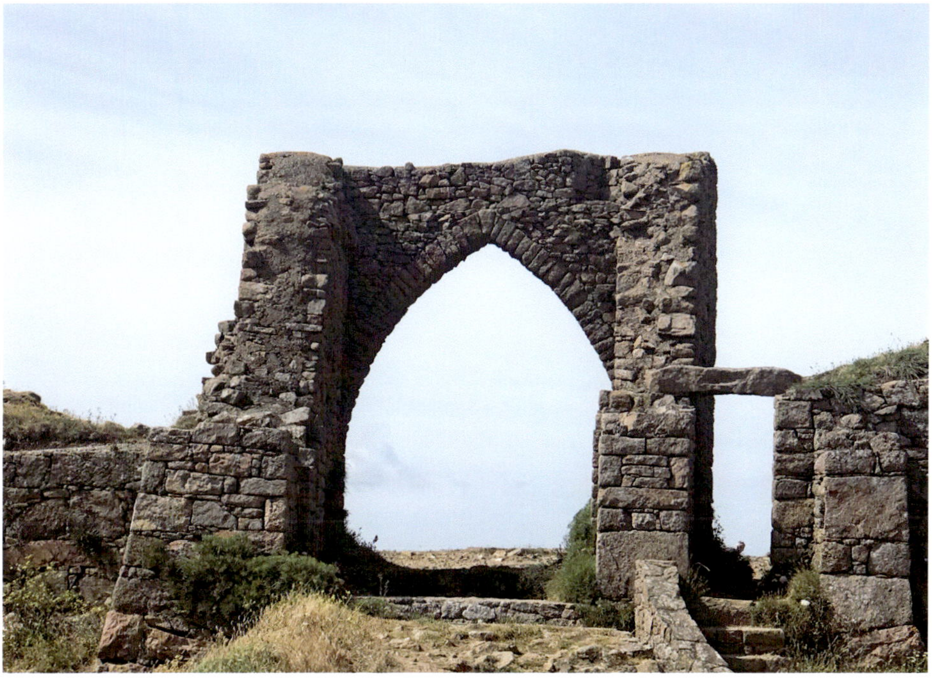

Archway at Grosnez Castle in St Ouen. (Author)

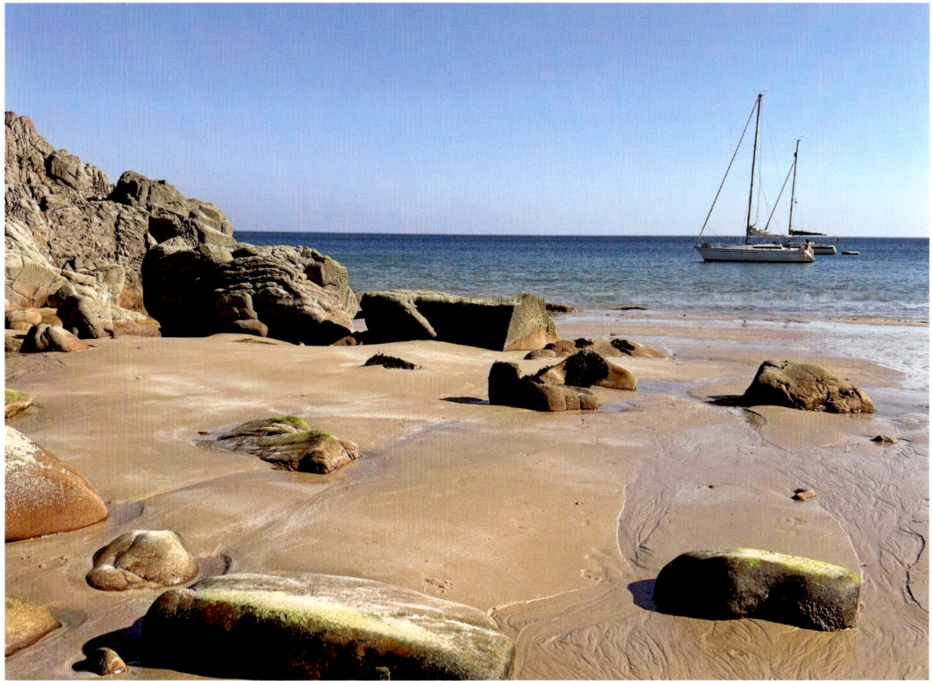

Beauport Bay. (Author)

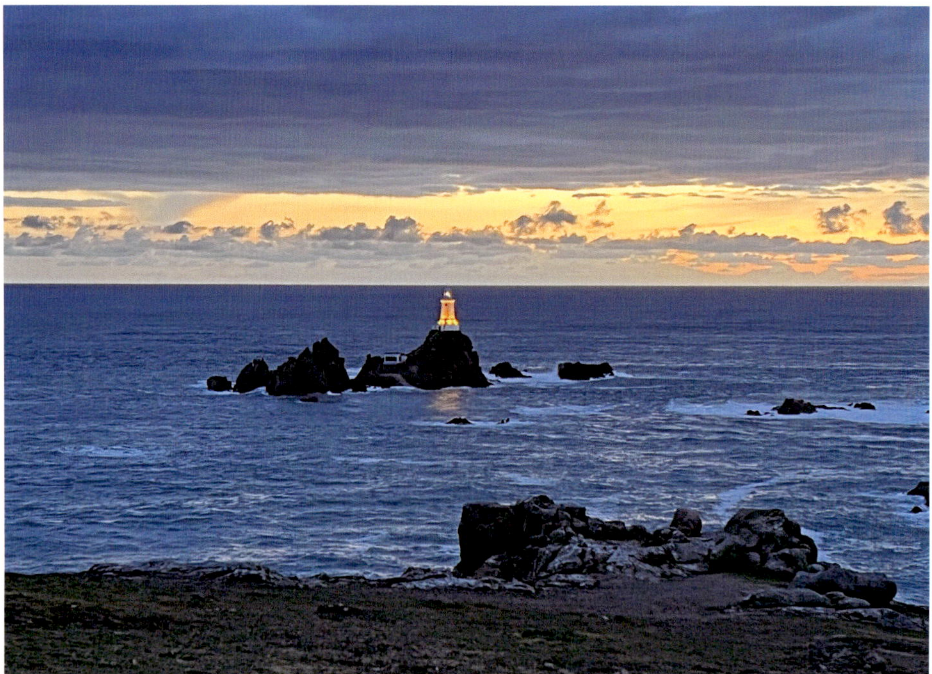

Corbière Lighthouse at sunset. (Author)

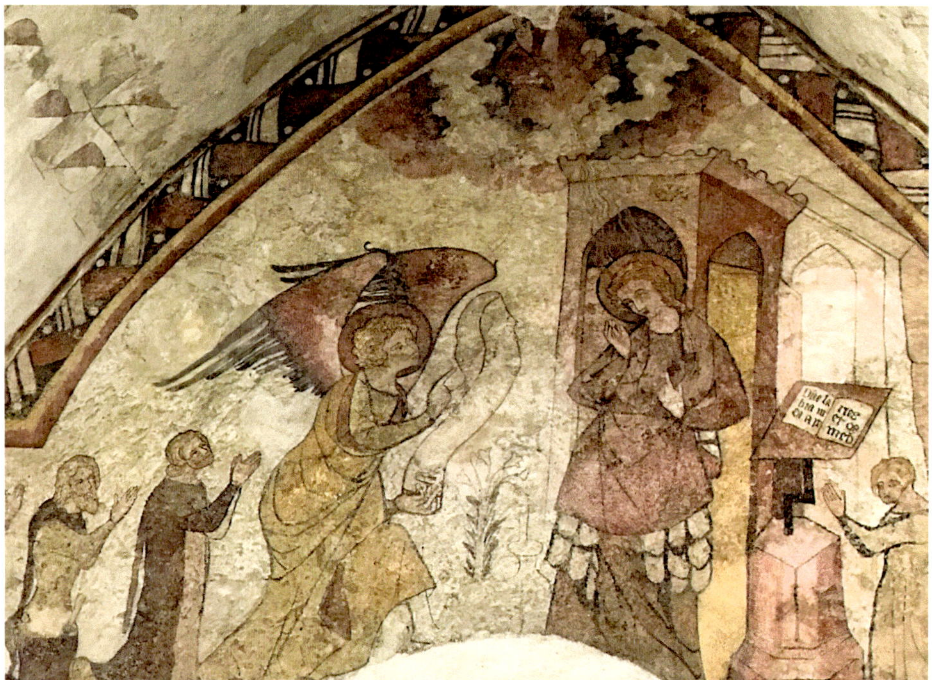

Detail from the Fishermen's Chapel at St Brelade's Church. (Author)

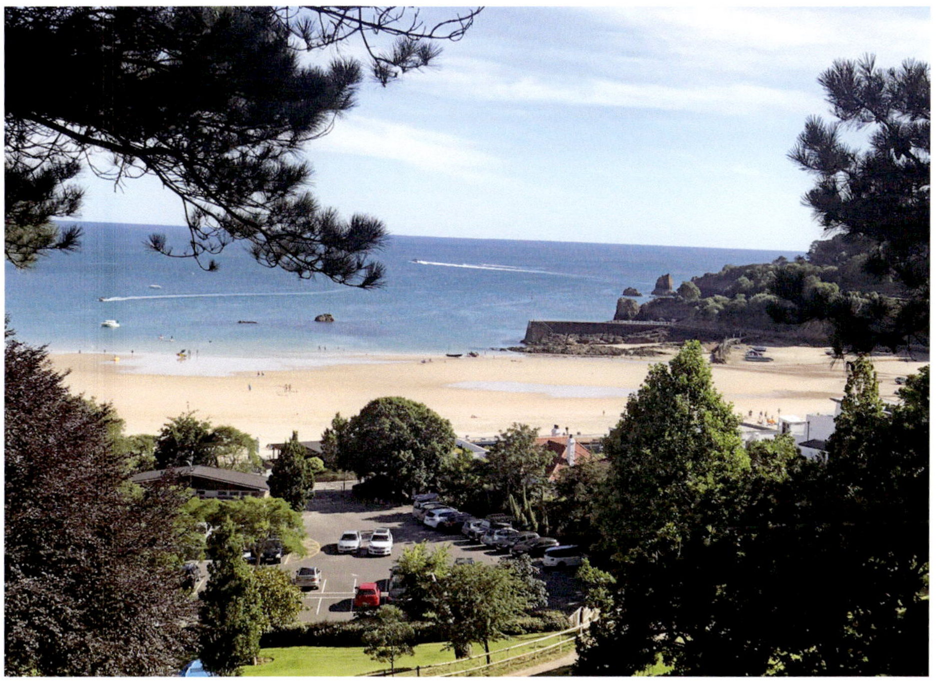

Looking down on St Brelade's Bay. (Author)

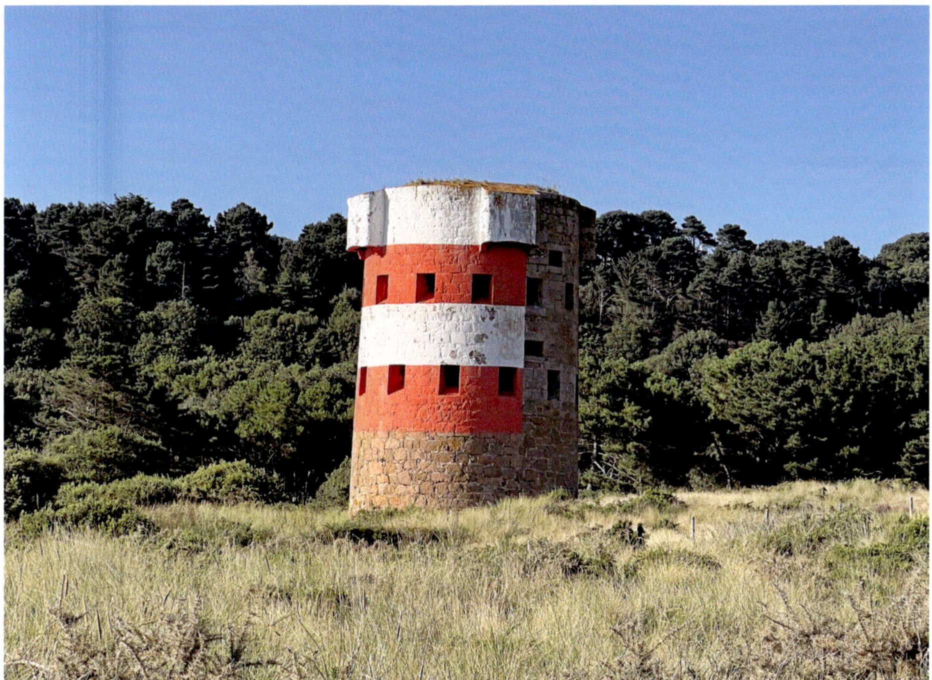

Ouaisné Tower in St Brelade. (Author)

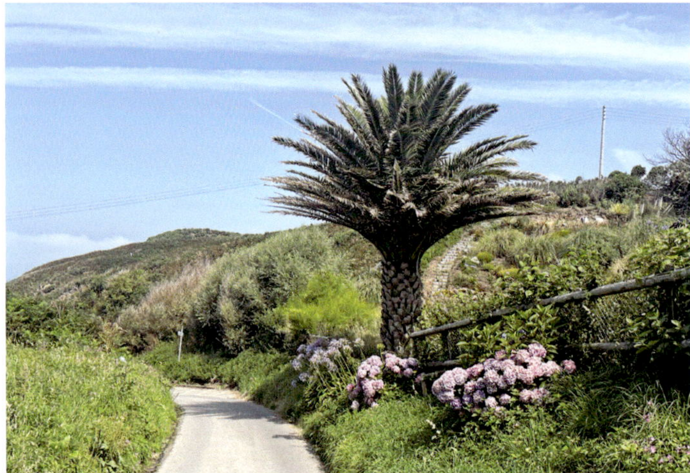

Plémont approach – palm tree. (Author)

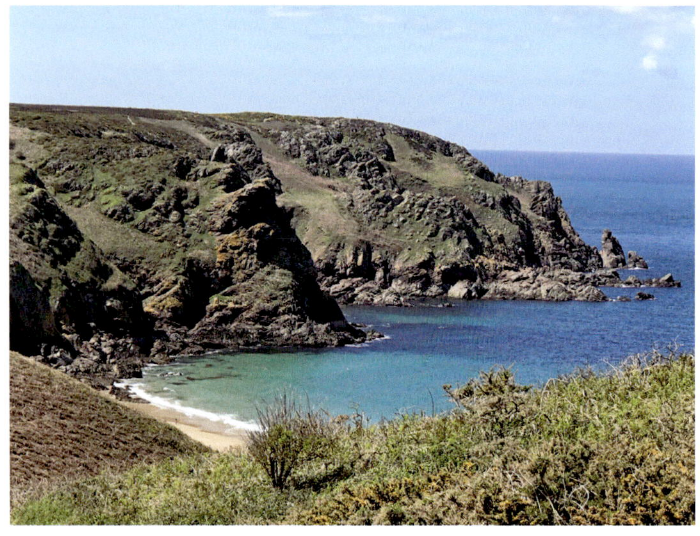

Plémont Bay. (Author)

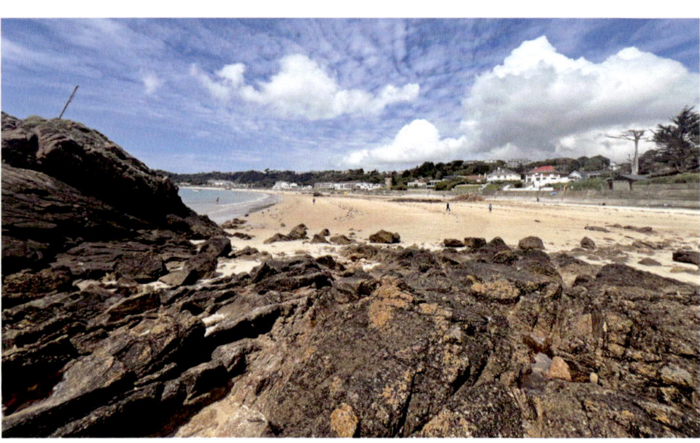

St Brelade's Bay seen from Ouaisné Bay. (Author)

The Lost Manor of La Brecquette

The ocean strikes Jersey from the west, as thousands of miles of cold Atlantic collide with the golden arc of St Ouen's Bay. There is nothing beyond but a limitless void of water, reaching all the way to the shores of Newfoundland. For medieval Jersey folk, this was truly the world's end, a place where the sky and sea fused. On summer nights, the sun melted like a candle on the horizon and hung in curtains of light, until darkness finally smothered it. Surely this place, they mused, was the threshold to Atlantis.

West of the great mount of l'Etacq, for half a mile or so right up to the water's edge, lay some of the fairest and richest *vergées* in Jersey. It was in these fortunate fields that Jean Wallis, Gentleman of Jersey, had his stronghold.

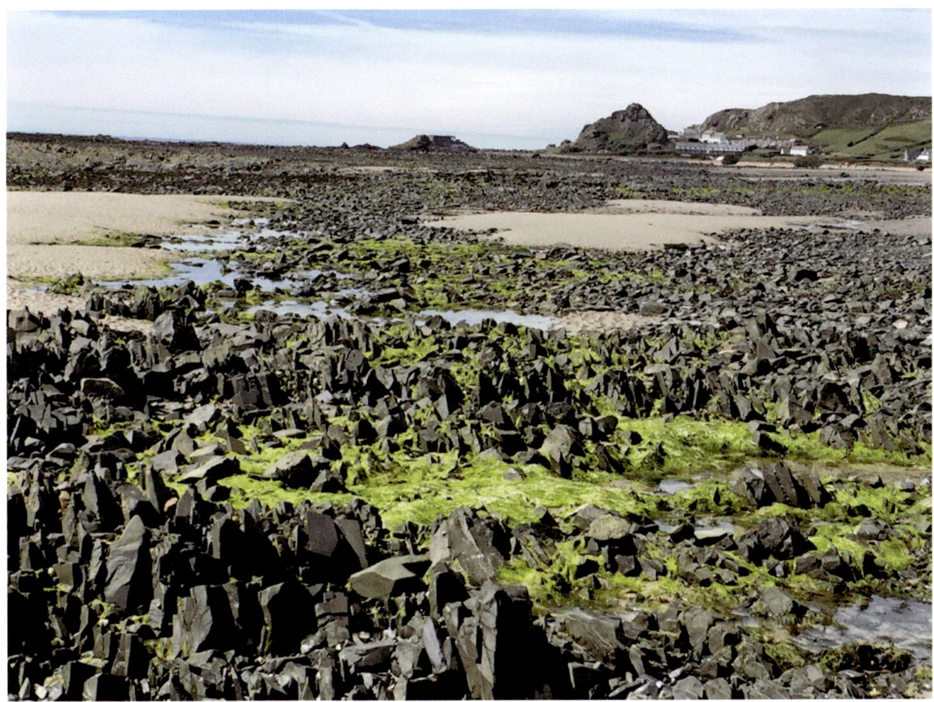

St Ouen's Bay near l'Etacq. (Author)

* * *

September 1356

The Watchman of La Brecquette Manor locked the gates as the autumn sun was swallowed up by the ocean. He began his nightly rounds by the great fountain, carrying a heavy iron lantern and a set of brass keys. The shadow of the keep loomed large against the blood-orange sunset.

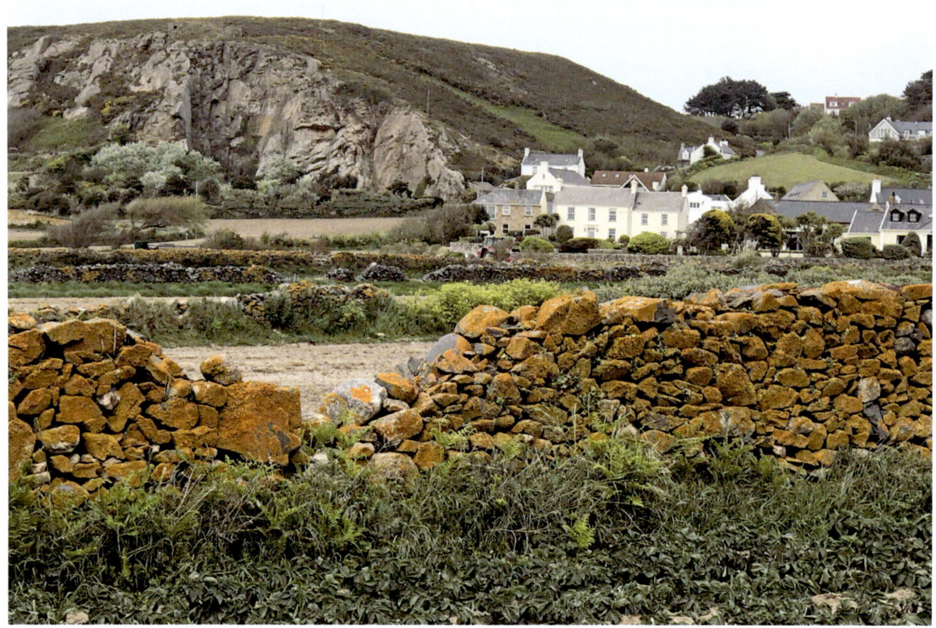

Le Chemin de la Brecquette in St Ouen. (Author)

The Manor of La Brecquette was a fortress in the Norman style, with heavy round *tourelles* and high walls of Jersey granite. It was flanked by an ancient oak forest, which had lingered from some forgotten time before the first men. The gnarled and mossy trees were bent double by centuries of Atlantic gales, hugging the earth, with vines and tendrils draped around them like curious creatures of the sea.

During the ages when the world was locked in ice, this flourishing forest had somehow survived, a remnant from an older world. The fields beyond, in this strange pocket of warmth, were astonishingly fertile, and the cider orchards yielded rich harvest. Jean Wallis, the Seigneur of the manor, was considered a wizard, an alchemist of sorts, for in autumn, the great stone presses turned apples into gold. Rumour had it that the manor's vaults concealed a king's ransom. The watchman knew the truth. His master Jean had drunk the cellars dry and squandered his good fortune. Scarcely a pouch of silver coins remained.

Jean Wallis was a shambling bear of a man, hospitable to a fault but prone to squalls of sudden rage. He had served the King with distinction on the battlefields of France. His weakness was his wine, and he was a regular drinking companion of Jean Mathurins, the Warden of the Isles, and Guille Hastein, the Bailiff. They would often feast together in the Great Hall of La Brecquette, regaling each other with battlefield tales, recounting their fleeting days of glory; three old men circling the dying embers of a fire, heads spinning with wine, oblivious to the rising tide.

Yet tonight Wallis would dine alone. The Warden had been summoned to Whitehall last month, and his ship had long since sailed. The Bailiff was in the great keep at Gorey tonight, dealing with matters in the eastern parishes. The Manor of La Brecquette slumbered. Smoke rose from the scullery, and a few stable-boys laughed and threw dice in the outhouses. The Watchman continued his lonely circuit of the castle walls.

He strode through the orchards, ripe and plump with fruit. The horses would soon be working *lé tou d'preinseu*, the stone apple crusher in the barn. The days would be hard but fruitful, with kegs of cider and wedges of black butter stored up for the feast days ahead.

The Watchman neared the boundary of the estate, the shore of the bay. It would be a high tide tonight, the highest of the year, and already he could see the waters racing up the sands, infiltrating gulleys, moving faster than a man could run. In recent years the sea had become more petulant, encroaching ever further, breaching sandbars and boldly reclaiming more and more manorial land. He prayed the earthern ramparts protecting the orchards would hold.

Then he saw it. A dark fist of cloud was rising in the twilight, a malevolent spiral over the ocean. A blaze of greenish yellow lightning danced silently on the horizon, fiery daggers stoking the waves to new heights. The air was electric now, and his robe crackled. A volley of fire and thunder suddenly rolled over the water. A great storm was heading into shore. All at once, the wind began to sing and howl and then knocked him to his knees.

The Watchman hastened back to the orchard, to raise the *clameur*, the traditional alarm. He took a bronze bell from his cloak and began to ring it, but the storm front was catching up with him. The sky began to spit, great gobbets of hail, nuggets of black ice. Then a spell seemed to break above the forest of La Brecquette.

He had rarely seen birds fly at night, but great flocks were rising around him in the forest and flying towards the interior of the Island. Even the doves in the colomberie were leaving the comfort of their perches and frantically launching themselves into the air. Every rat and mouse and squirrel was rustling at his feet, as if a secret command had broken their slumbers and sent them racing to higher ground. The lord's hounds were battering frantically at the doors of their kennel; they pushed past the sleepy stable-boys and leaped away in the direction of l'Etacq. Then came a thunderous juggernaut as a stable door slammed hard to the ground. The lord's horses, the most dutiful and docile of all beasts, had bolted.

The Watchman stood at the castle gates, as the full fury of the storm broke. He fumbled with the heavy brass keys and entered the warm air of the Great Hall. Lavish tapestries were draped from the wall here, beside gilt candelabras and a magnificent, smouldering fireplace. Jean Wallis lay slumped in his chair, his cheeks flush with wine, a plate of prime beef uneaten on the bench before him. The Watchman shook him and tried to wake him, but to no avail. He was

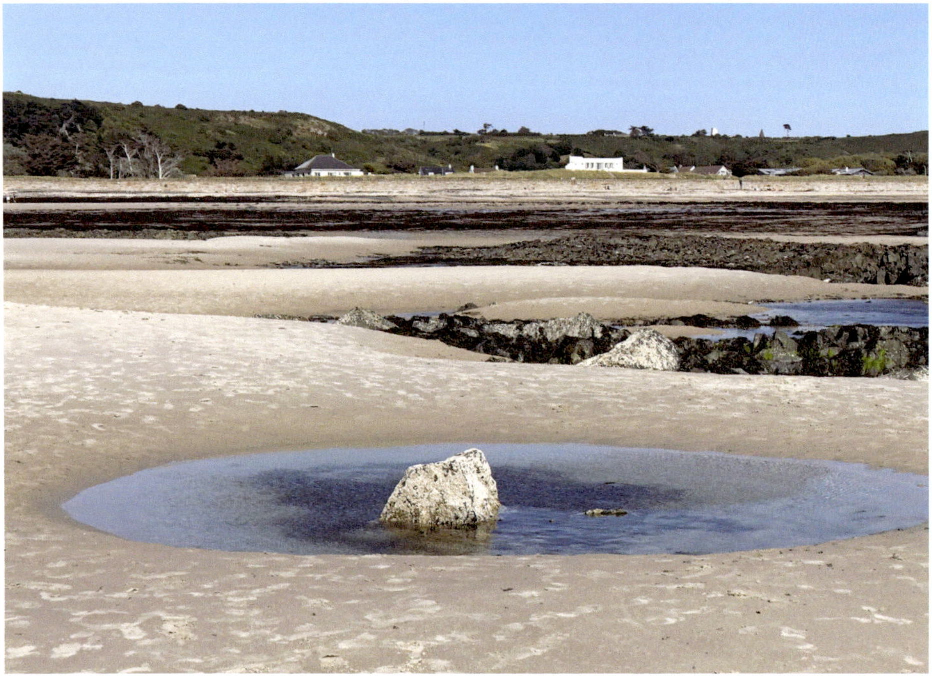

St Ouen's Bay near La Brecquette slipway. (Author)

prisoned as if by a fatal enchantment. He was a corpulent man, too great to carry, so the Watchman needed to summon help from the servants.

He was heading for the scullery to find them when the burst of a hurricane sent him reeling. The violent storm was laying waste to the castle, lashing at its *tourelles*, sending tiles flying into the yard. The west tower was quaking under the impact and its peak began to crumble in a funnel of masonry and dust. Saltwater was rising at his feet too, bursting up through the fountain in the yard. The ground was turning into a mire.

Then his heart exploded. A hundred yards out, he saw an enormous wall of churning water, punching through the earthworks and ripping apple trees from the soft earth. With every breaking wave, the seething sea pressed closer. The Watchman dropped his lantern and ran for his life through the field of La Haussière. Fear lent him wings, and he was soon climbing the rock of l'Etacq, plunging through the gorse bushes, seeking the higher ground.

A monstrous wave was brewing behind him, the seventh of seven, of a magnitude unseen before or since. Turning back, the Watchman saw the waterspout of the storm break upon the manor house, and the *tourelles* tumbling like dice. For a moment, a black blade of water hung over the castle like an executioner's axe. He stared dumbfounded as it began to drop, and after that he remembered no more.

* * *

The Watchman awoke where the waves had left him marooned on the Rock of l'Etacq. He was drenched and shivering in the pale pink light of dawn. The storm had gone, and the tide had receded. He could see that the sea had carved an utterly new boundary with the land. Jersey was truncated, and the field of La Haussière had now become the beach. The entire fief of La Brecquette – manor house and orchards all – had been struck from the face of creation. The keys he clasped were a doorway to Atlantis, a portal to a drowned kingdom.

The castle of La Brecquette had been torn down, stone by stone. Salvage men came searching later that day for bodies, but none were ever found. When the tide returned that afternoon, it submerged every remnant of the old castle. A few foundation stones remained, but within a year even these had been plundered for their valuable granite. The Watchman had lost everyone and everything that he was charged to defend.

* * *

La Brecquette faded into legend; a powerful emblem of mutability and fate. Scoured by the waves, forever lost. Fragments of memory persisted. In 1669, in a lawsuit on manorial boundaries, depositions were taken on the manor's presumed location, but already it was a matter of conjecture and hearsay. Even today, on the very lowest tides, the remnants of an ancient, drowned forest are revealed. With enough imagination, a ledge of undersea rock might pass as the foundation of a medieval hall, where a mighty lord once feasted. For a few fleeting hours, we catch glimpses of a drowned world, but then the tide turns with a vengeance, and the ocean reclaims its own.

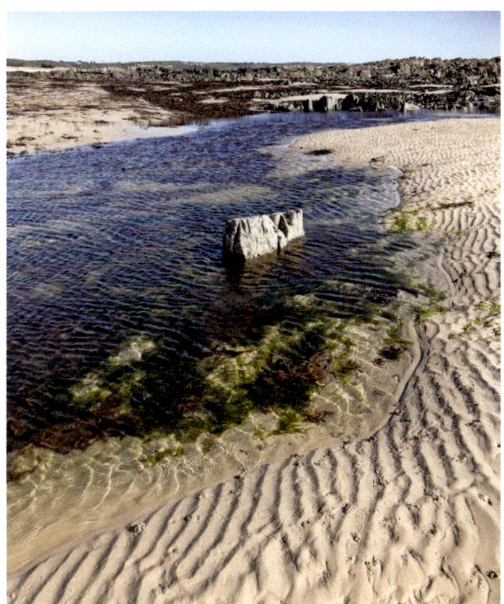

St Ouen's Bay near the reputed site of the Lost Manor. (Author)

De Carteret's Leap

For almost 900 years, the de Carteret family have held the lordship, or Seigneurie, of St Ouen's Manor. This is an ancient and beautiful fortress and a worthy ancestral seat for Jersey's largest parish. Yet in the 1460s, with England riven by the Wars of the Roses, the Seigneur of St Ouen found himself in a perilous position. Jersey was captured by a French army in May 1461, and it would be seven years before King Edward IV's fleet successfully reconquered the Island. The legend of de Carteret's leap, which may have some historical foundation, dates from this turbulent era of French occupation.

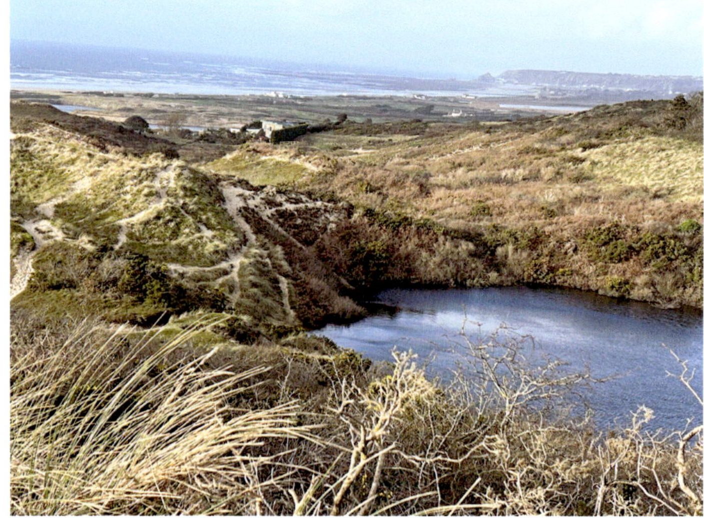

Les Mielles looking
west towards
St Ouen's Bay.
(Author)

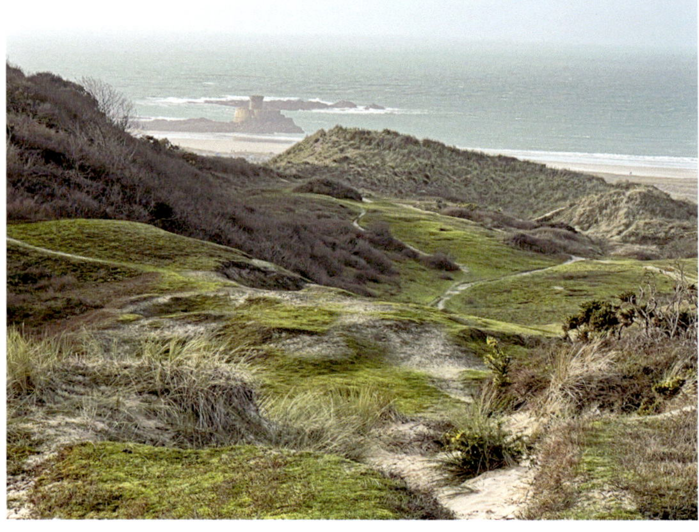

Looking at
St Ouen's Bay
from Les Mielles.
(Author)

Philippe de Carteret, St Ouen's Pond, Jersey, September 1467
The summer sun was dying in the western sky. Philippe de Carteret watched as the disc of reddish copper plunged into the ocean, and the darkness raced to meet him over the sands.

The grizzled Seigneur of St Ouen lingered on the edge of the dunes awhile longer, lost in the depths of his thoughts. He was tall and vigorous, not yet forty years old, yet a man ageing before his time. His shoulders carried the burden of cares too heavy to measure. His face was riven by scars, for he had fought too hard for too long.

Philippe stood on wounded ground. Barely a century before, a storm had drowned the nearby manor of La Brecquette and scoured the very foundations clean. His father had told him the story many times, of the day the great wave came. Tides can turn so suddenly, he noted, fortunes may change, and many who are now great will later be swallowed up by the sand.

It was a portent of the world to come. In recent years, England had been torn apart by civil war, as the white and red roses of York and Lancaster clashed like duelling dragons, seeking to devour each other. A single flick of their tails had been enough to cast Jersey into the abyss.

The Island proved an ideal bargaining chip, a toy to be traded between princes. The Lancastrian queen had slipped the keys to the French. Through ruse and treachery, a postern gate left ajar at Gorey Castle, the wolf had been let in through the door. His name was the Count of Maulevrier, and he was the new Lord of

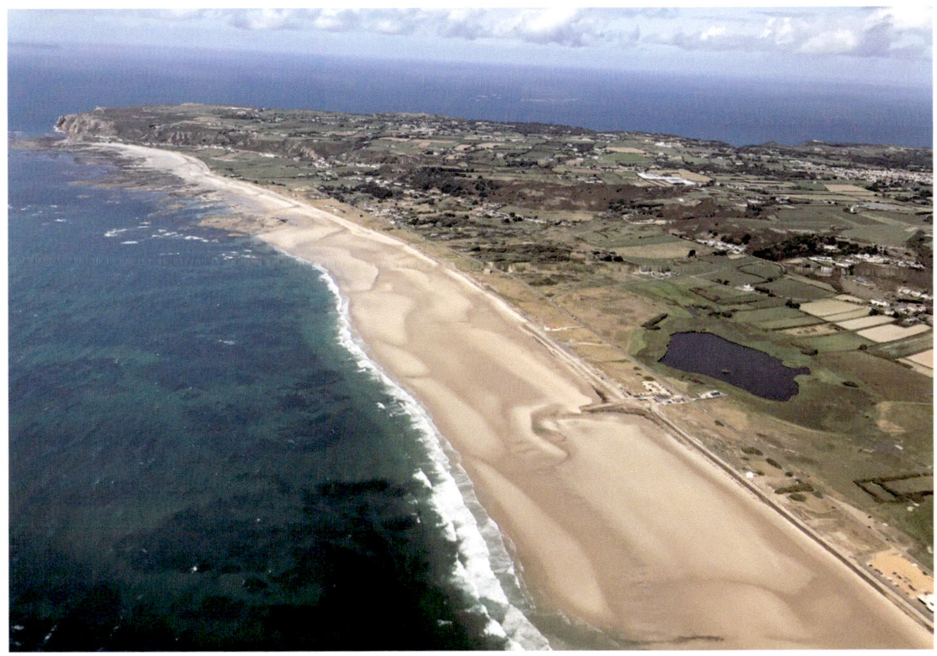

St Ouen's Bay from the air – with St Ouen's Pond in the foreground. (Author)

the Isles. His warlords roamed the parishes without restraint, rustling sheep like vagabonds, plundering without quarter.

There was only one stumbling block to his unfettered power: the lone man staring at the setting sun. Philippe de Carteret was the scion of an ancient line of Jersey nobility. To be sure, a determined army might dislodge him from his bastion, his heavily fortified manor house of St Ouen. Yet the price in blood and treasure would be high, for Philippe commanded the fierce loyalty of the West. Some subtler ruse would be needed to bring him to heel.

Even as the Count seethed with anger, correct chivalric form insisted that a pretence of cordiality should be maintained. The Seigneur and his wife dined with the occupation army at Mont Orgueil; honour was upheld. Yet it was an open secret that Philippe's true fealty lay with the English crown. His days of safety were numbered, as surely as the hourglass slipped towards sunset.

* * *

Philippe turned back to his manorial pond, silvery and smooth as a mirror. He had spent a full day fishing, hoping that the simple rhythm of line and hook could ease his troubled mind. Now the catch was in, the day was done. So, he lobbed a stone into the water, watching the ripples on the pond spread and diminish, until they were finally gone. Like life itself, he mused; drama and passion, fading to black. The lake lay as still as the night.

Philippe's black steed paced softly behind him on the shoreline, a handsome war horse. The French name for his kind was a *destrier*: a horse powerful beyond measure, foremost among his kind. He had been Philippe's faithful companion for years and seen his fair share of combat.

Suddenly, the great horse whinnied: a terrifying and unmistakeable cry of fear. Philippe threw aside his fishing pole and leapt to his feet. In an instant, he sprang up onto the saddle, reaching for his sword, ready to face the imminent threat. It was almost too late.

Armed men were rising from the sands, daggers drawn, ready to seize him, or cleave him in two if he resisted. There must have been nine or ten of them, French soldiers, bristling with knives. Their leader brandished a coil of rope, the better to bind their prisoner. The ambush had been sprung.

The odds were impossible. Philippe spurred his horse, charging across the sands, up and away from the pond, making for the higher ground. It was not an easy flight; the dunes were steep and treacherous, riddled with snares, a natural defensive barrier that protected the Island from the west.

As if in a dream, he rode for the hills, but his lead was slender. The French soldiers had mounted their own chargers. It was evident that these were no common men-at-arms but highly trained knights; the Count had sent his finest riders.

Philippe fled for his life. He felt his horse's heart exploding as he galloped up the slope, but he dared not ease off for a moment. The Seigneur could already glimpse the rondel tower of his manor house over the horizon, the promise of safety so tantalisingly close. Yet as he crested the hill, a flight of arrows burst above him. Instinctively, he swerved. The bank of arrows ripped into a nearby bank of gorse, burying their heads in the sand.

Philippe had raced straight into a trap. Too late: he saw a hedgehog of halberds bristling at the brow of the hill, a second detachment of soldiers to block him. The Seigneur lurched away and rode hard to the right, desperate to evade them before the jaws of the ambush closed. With a sinking heart, he realised he was trapped.

The land fell sharply away ahead, into a deep wooded valley – *Le Val de la Charrière* they called it, a chasm of 18 feet, three times the height of a man. If he fell into the bushes below, he would be easy meat. The kidnappers were close on his heels now, steel glinting in the twilight, eager to catch their prey. A void of 22 feet separated him from safety, an angel's leap.

The lone rider committed his soul to God. Then, with a desperate burst of power, Philippe spurred his horse and leapt into empty space. The chasm reached forward to swallow him up.

There was a strange moment of falling as the sun died over the sea. For a moment all was frozen around him: the troop of angry, armoured riders; the horizon burning up at sunset; the green gorse and sand and sea. The stink of sweat flooded his nostrils, rising from the mane of an exhausted black horse; a horse now in mid-leap, hurtling through the air.

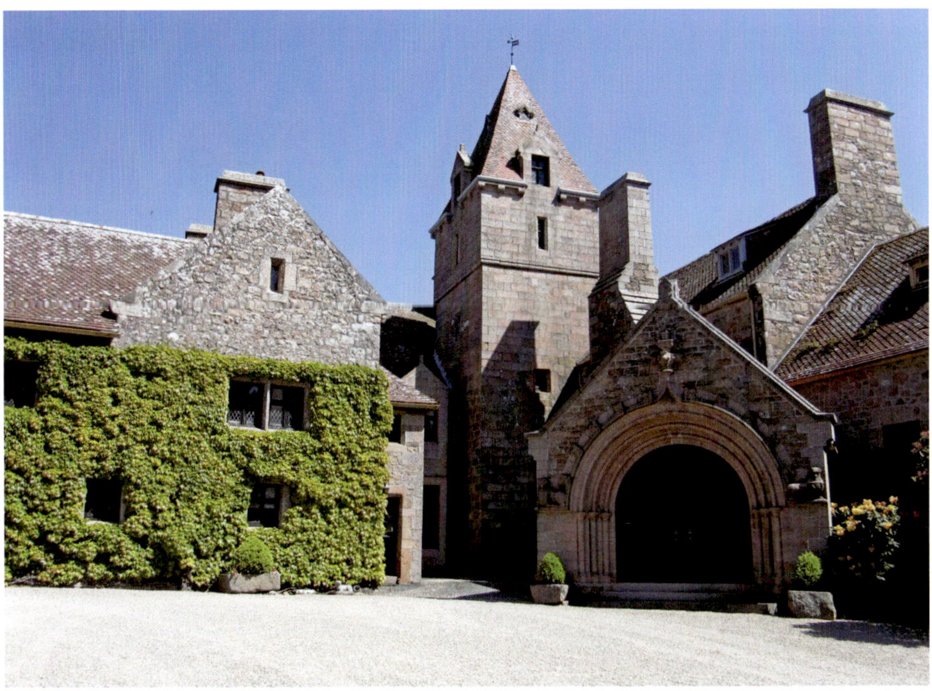

St Ouen's Manor. (Author, used courtesy of St Ouen's Manor)

Like Pegasus, the horse flew. Then his forelegs struck solid earth, stumbling for grip. He struggled for a moment, but he did not fall. He charged on. At last, the strong walls of the manor were in sight. Lanterns burned on the battlements, beckoning them home.

Horse and rider burst free and clear into the yard. Philippe leapt up as the horse's forelegs crumpled, and his body slumped to the earth. Overcome by emotion, he embraced his beloved steed, calming him as his lifeblood ebbed into the sandy soil. Then his men-at-arms rushed to meet him, ushering him to safety behind the iron gates of the stronghold. Far away in the night, his dejected foes slunk away, retreating to the east, their plot foiled.

This impossible leap of a faithful steed had changed the fate of an island. The people would never succumb to the invader, and in time the occupiers were driven out and Jersey returned to the fold of the English crown. The horse's sacrifice was solemnly remembered. Philippe de Carteret, mourning his loyal steed, ordered that it be buried with honour in a spot right beneath the walls of his fortress.

***

The legend of the black horse of de Carteret lived on, a tale of valour passed down the generations. It was immortalised in a great painting, hanging with pride of place in the Manor. Some considered it a medieval fable, a mere allegory or symbol. In the centuries to come, it was regularly retold in the guidebooks, a charming fable to amuse Victorian tourists. Perhaps it was just a child's whisper, a fairy tale, nothing more.

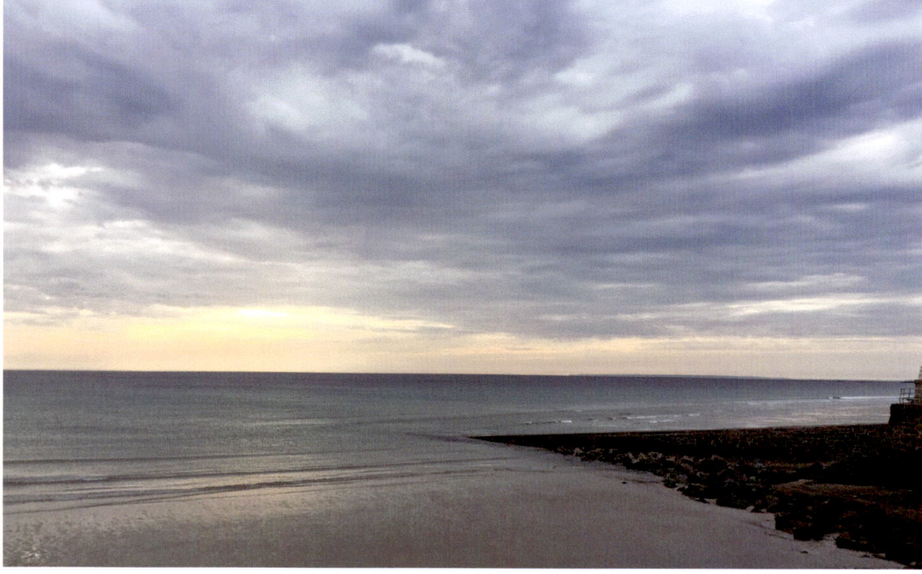

St Ouen's Bay – looking to infinity. (Author)

Then, at the dawn of the twentieth century, routine excavations took place in the Manor grounds, digging the foundations for a walled garden. At the very spot recounted in the ancient myth, something curious was unearthed. The labourers were puzzled until they remembered an ancient story. They had discovered the bones of a great and noble steed.

Janvrin's Tomb

Portelet Bay, set on the south coast of the western parish of St Brélade, is perhaps the quintessential Jersey beach. An idyllic tidal islet is connected to the beach by a golden sandbar: it is a sublime location. Generations of holidaymakers have flocked here, yet few are aware of the personal tragedy associated with this idyllic bay. The tale opens in the summer of 1721, as the trading ship *Esther* is returning from a lucrative expedition to France. Her homecoming is not destined to be a happy one.

Captain Philippe Janvrin, *The Esther*, Belcroute Bay, Jersey, September 1721
Death crept into Europe on a bright spring morning, draped in the finest of silks. By the time the *Grand-Saint-Antoine* docked in Marseilles, its sailors were already pale and listing, as frail as old men. The harbourmaster quarantined the ship, isolating it in the 'lazaret' dock until the foul humours blew over, and the seasons turned afresh.

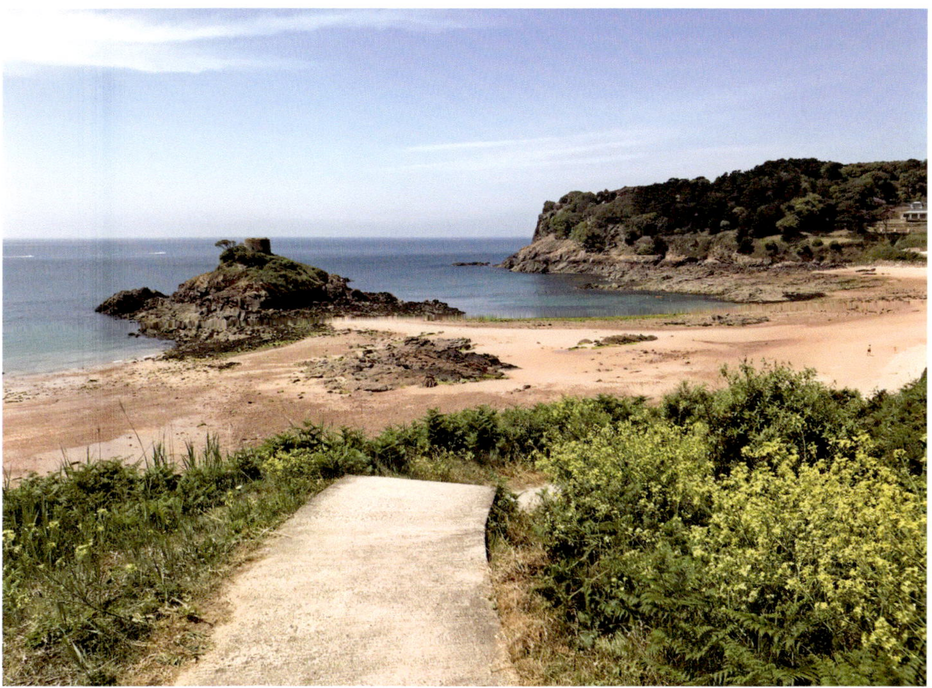

Portelet Bay. (Author)

Yet the city fathers coveted the silks, thick and plush and lavish, that lay within its hold. Eyes bulging with greed, they overruled the sanitation board and commanded its wares to be unloaded at once. It was a fatal decision. Within days, a fierce pestilence burned through the French city like wildfire. The people were sickening fast, their limbs horrifically swelling, and the graveyards were soon overflowing with corpses.

Too late, the authorities realised their grievous error. In desperation, the King of France and the Pope ordered a plague wall to be built – the *mur de peste* – to seal off the afflicted region. This defence was soon breached, a feeble sandcastle in the face of the incoming tide.

***

The news of the advancing plague fell like a shroud over the taverns of St Aubin and the counting-houses of St Helier. I shivered when I first heard the stories, for I am captain of the trading ship *Esther*, and France is my backyard. The sea will not shield us from her fate.

***

Jersey lies fearfully exposed, bound to the Continent by bonds of blood and money. We are an island of sharp-eyed traders, the sea pulsing in our veins and a dozen deals jostling in our head. We merchants are jugglers of costs and margins, quick to calculate *livres* and *sous*, able to sell our wares in any port. Our secret is simple: we provide exactly what the French desire; namely gorgeous woollen stockings, whose provenance is a byword for quality. Indeed, our Island and its knitwear are one and the same in the customer's mind; they call our produce 'jerseys'. We repay the geographical homage, and cart home fat barrels of 'Bordeaux'.

Summer would soon be ending. We risked one final, precious sally down to France, unloading our cargo at Nantes and stuffing our hold with a last batch of wine to carry home. It felt as if we had stumbled across a city of the night. Inns were bolted shut; doors were locked and barred. Solemn bells tolled above the rooftops, and priests directed the parades of coffins along the streets. This was a city cowering in its cloisters, a land that had gone to seed. I witnessed hordes of black rats, as fat as piglets, gorging themselves on the grain in the dockside storehouses.

The customs and formalities dragged tediously on, due to the want of men, and my crew grew hot and restless. At last, we weighed anchor, relieved to be heading home to Jersey, into the arms of my wife Elizabeth. Yet as we crawled down the Loire estuary towards the Bay of Biscay, my forehead was already drenched in sweat.

By our second night at sea, I was bedridden. As we approached Jersey, I was weakening fast. Now my ship lies quarantined by Belcroute Bay, beside the bleak shingle beach and the dark, wooded cliffs.

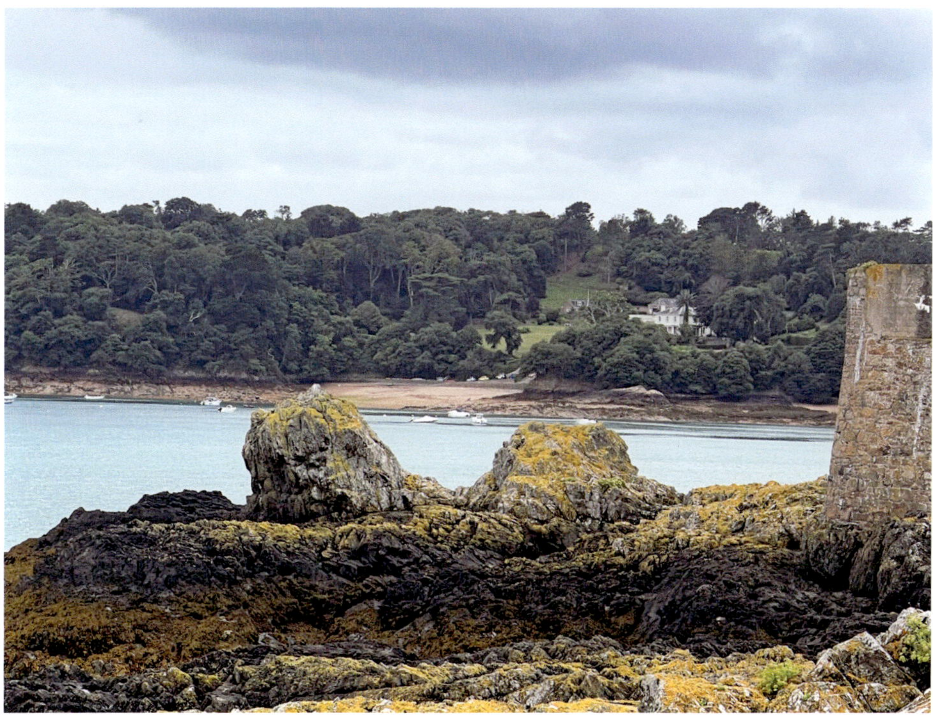

A view of Belcroute Bay seen from St Aubin's Fort. (Author)

My wife and children have been forbidden to visit me; even the crew tiptoe outside my cabin in hoods, leaving food and water by the door. I am burning up in a terrible fever, and my armpits are swollen and black. I was a fool to set out on this fatal venture, and I will die here alone rather than risk the lives of those I love. Jersey must be spared from my inevitable fate; that is all that matters to me now.

The hour has come. The dying sun slips behind Noirmont, and the ship hangs in the darkness. Elizabeth's prayers whisper in my ears, and moonlight falls upon the water. Through the porthole, I see the lights of St Aubin, scattered like stars across the bay. Somewhere beneath them is everything I love, everything I have known, everything that I now must leave behind.

** * **

Captain Philippe Janvrin died that night. He was forty-four years old. His sacrifice in submitting to isolation to protect his beloved Island was not in vain. Aboard the *Esther*, the fever soon burned itself out, and the shadow of infection lifted from Jersey. The terror of the bubonic plague would soon fade from the pages of history.

Elizabeth Janvrin, bereft with grief, petitioned the Lieutenant-Governor to allow her husband a Christian burial. The authorities looked upon her with pity, but they were fearful to carry the body ashore. Instead, they decided Captain Janvrin should be laid to rest on the remote tidal islet of Ile au Guerdain, nestled in the heart of Portelet Bay. On the twenty-seventh day of September, three sailors rowed his body to this rocky outcrop and scrambled up to its summit. Then Janvrin's plague-ravaged body was lowered into his lonely tomb.

The sailors gave a signal, and the funeral service began. The Reverend Philip Messervy, Rector of St Brélade, officiated divine service from the hilltop, as the parishioners remembered one of their own. From that day on they would call it Janvrin's Tomb, set high upon the rock, joined to the shore at low tide by an isthmus of golden sand.

Some say his body was eventually exhumed and re-interred in the ancient church of St Brélade. Yet no one can say for sure. Though the dreaded plague had gone, revolution and war would follow in the century to come. In the fearful days of Napoleon, the tomb was covered up by a military tower, built to defend the bay. A small detachment of soldiers bunkered down on the desolate rock, waiting for an invasion that never came. In a still later age, the bay would become a much-loved holiday beach, a cradle of childhood memories.

The name of Janvrin's Tomb endures, remembering the plague ship and the sacrifice of its captain. Twice daily the tides encircle his grave, sweeping in across the sands, running homewards towards the shore.

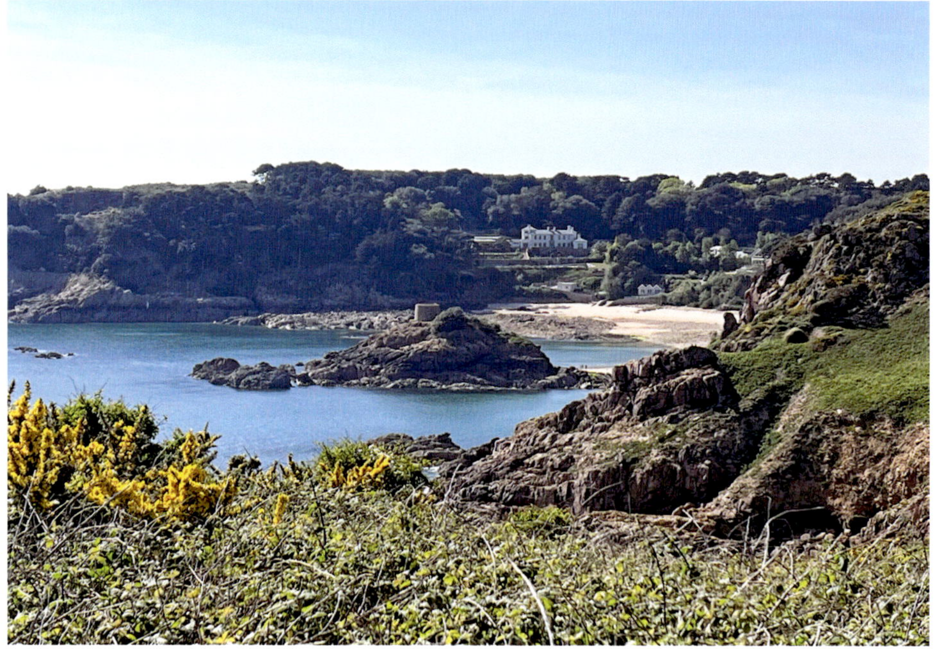

View of Portelet Bay from Portelet Common. (Author)

Tales of the North Coast

The north coast of Jersey is a world apart. In the parish of Trinity, sheer cliffs plunge 400 feet down to the sea. The waters are deeper here, and safe landing places are few. Its densely wooded shores have offered a haven to vagabonds and smugglers over the centuries. These medieval tales are both set in Bouley Bay, a tiny harbour set beside some of the steepest cliffs in Jersey. The fears they reveal are primal – of the threat lurking somewhere beyond the fireside, of the need to shun the cliffs after nightfall. Of course, not all would heed the warnings.

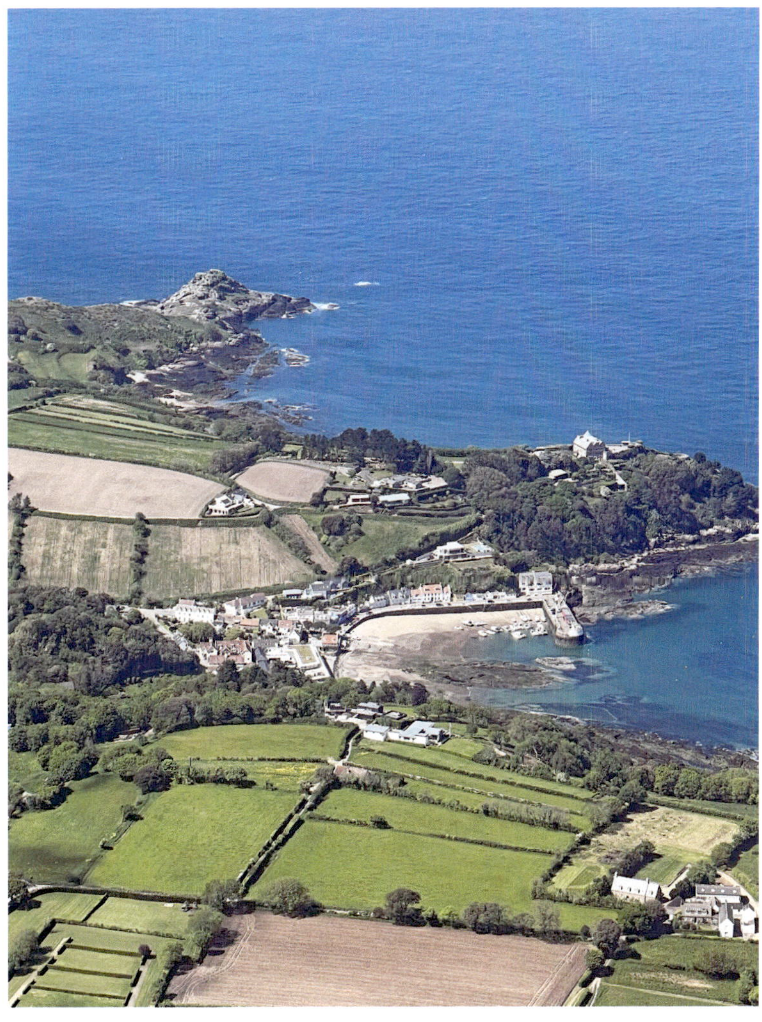

Aerial view of Rozel. (Author)

 Illustrated Tales of Jersey

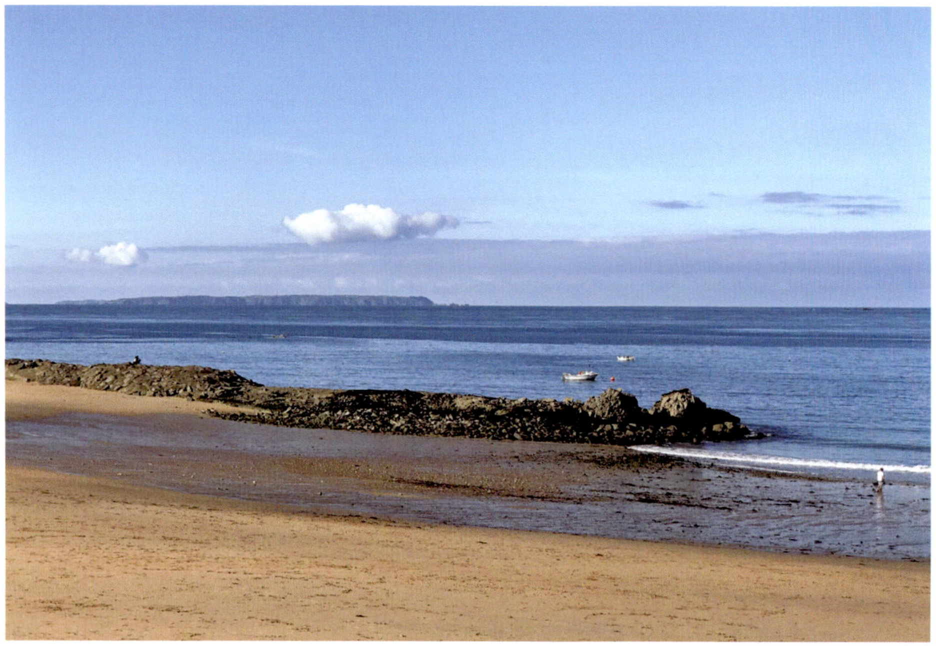

Grève de Lecq with Sark on the horizon. (Author)

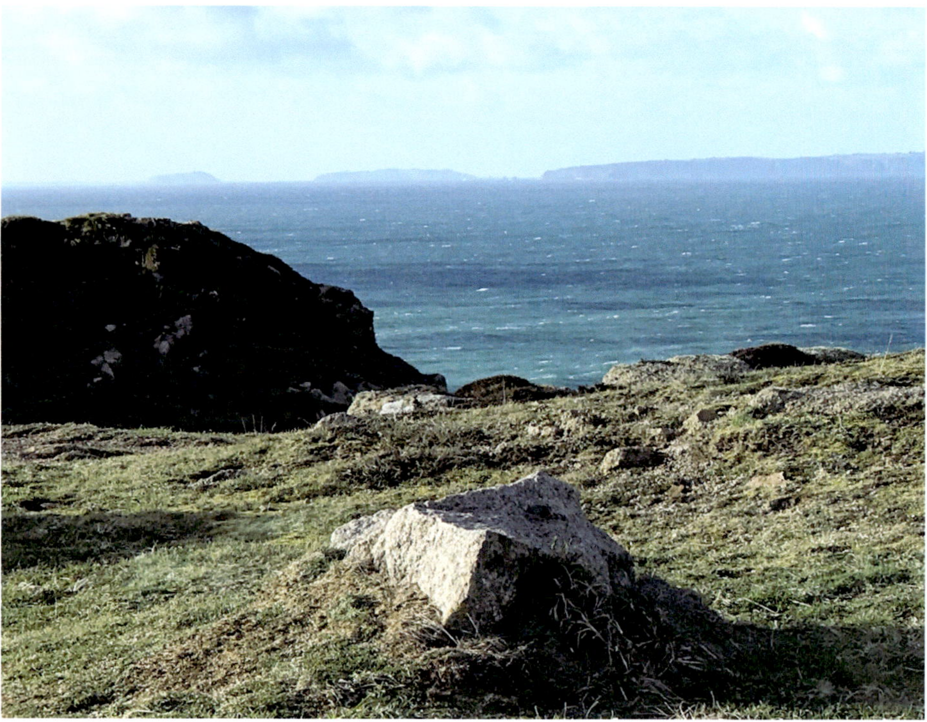

Looking north towards Sark. (Author)

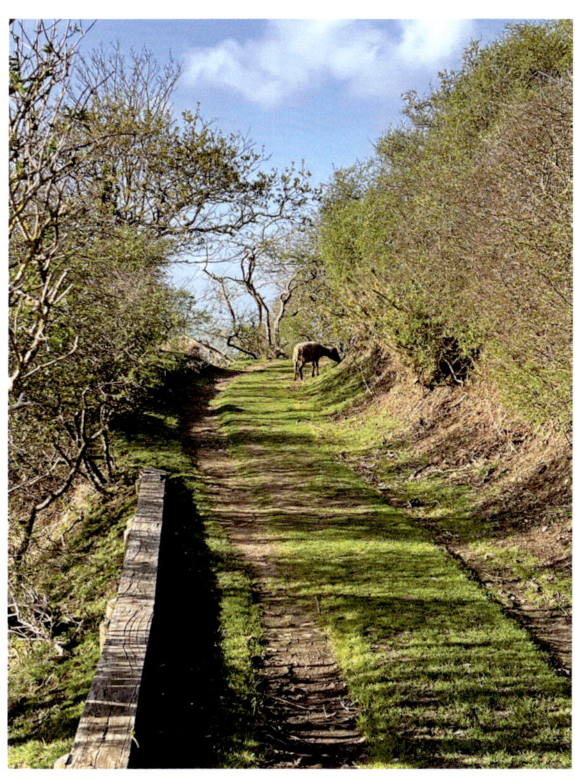

Right: North coast cliff path. (Author)

Below: Rock pools at Grève de Lecq. (Author)

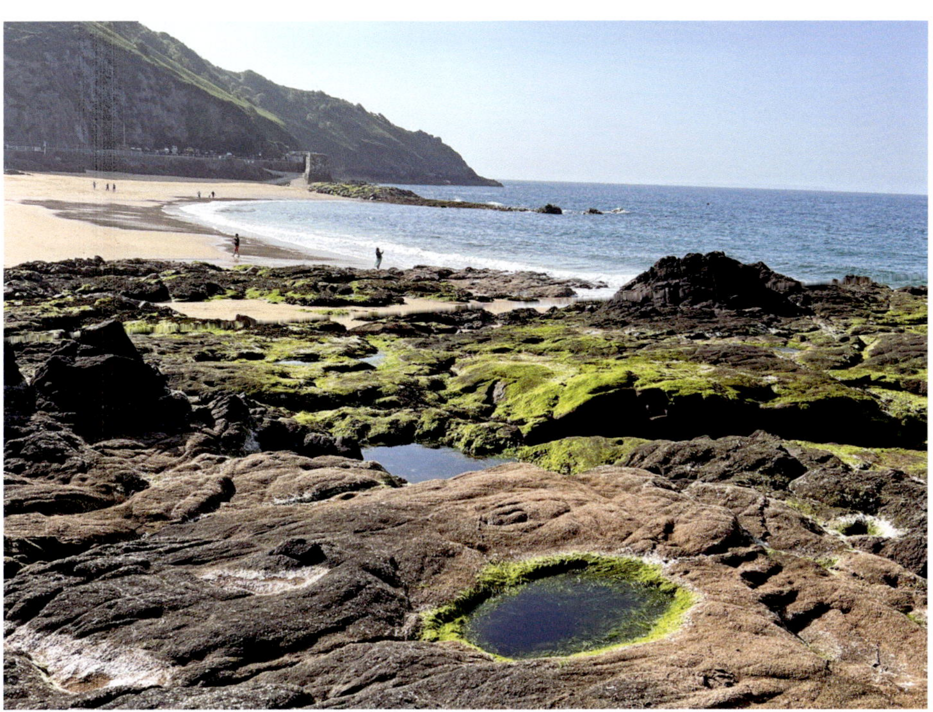

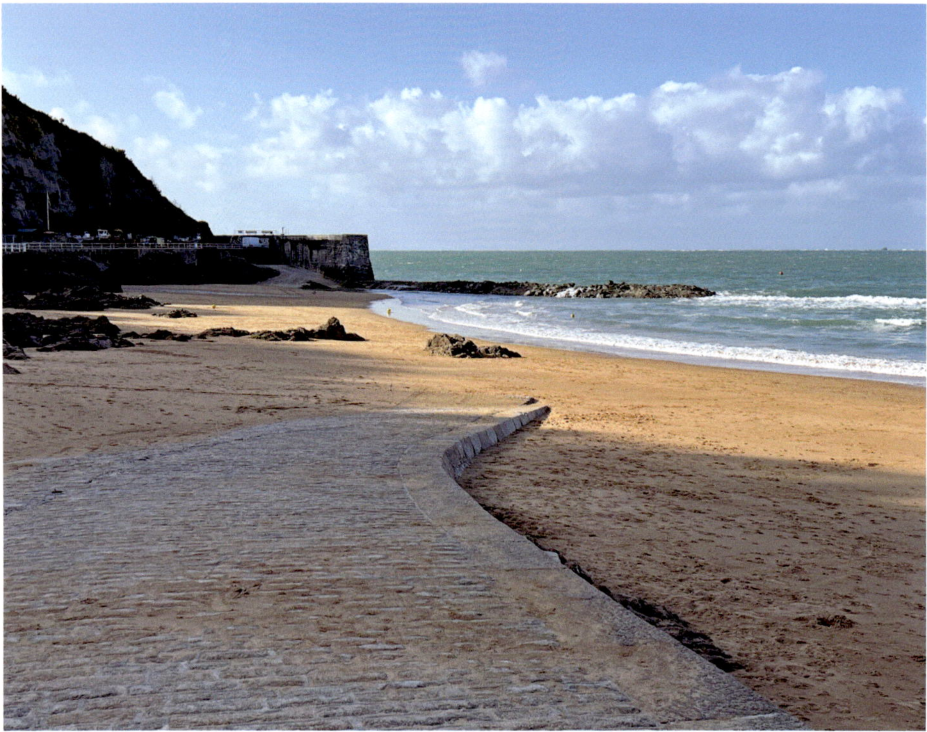

Slipway at Grève de Lecq. (Author)

Les Cris des Tombelènes: A Medieval Tragedy

Bouley Bay, Jersey, Autumn 1462

September ended with storms. The shortening days flickered past like a parade of guttering candles, and the people of Trinity cowered in their hovels. They said the sheep-stealers were riding harder now, emboldened by the darkening nights.

These were evil days. Abetted by treachery, the King of France had conquered Jersey, and his fleur-de-lys banner hung over Mont Orgueil. The administration of justice had ground to a halt, and the Warden of the Isles had fled. Armed gangs of criminals – deserters, irregulars, vagabonds – roamed the countryside on horseback. They rustled sheep, gorged on the fat of the land, and filled their boots with whatever they could kill for.

Yet even in these darkest hours, love and life would not be forsaken. One night, at the head of Bouley Bay, smoke drifted up into the night, for a betrothal feast was at hand. In these straitened times, it was rare enough to see any *Assise de Veille*, any snatched feast of celebration.

Tonight, the halls of Farmer Raulin's house were decked with the flowers of the forest: St John's herb, heather, the last blooms of late summer. A crowd of friends and well-wishers from the parish of the Holy Trinity had gathered there to greet a newly engaged couple. A feast was served in their honour, and fat barrels of cider

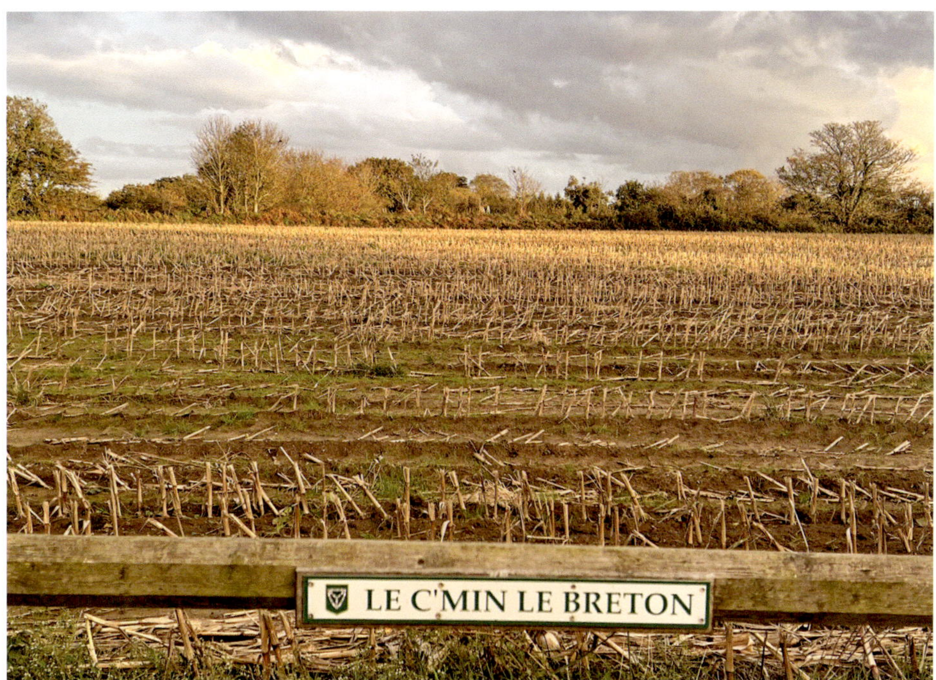

A Trinity field in autumn. (Author)

were split open. They had been scrupulously hoarded for such a time as this, a final fling before the bleak onset of winter.

For Old Farmer Raulin's only son and heir, the younger Raulin, had pledged his troth to Jeanne du Jourdain, maiden of the parish. Her eyes glinted green beside him in the firelight, smitten with love. The betrothal guests shovelled clumps of *vraic* onto the fire, and it crackled and burned ever brighter.

The revels were ending now, a ceremony crowned by a song. After much cajoling and persuasion, the shy bridegroom-to-be burst into voice. It was a *chanson* in pure and melodious Jersey French, a song of love and beauty and hope. His beloved melted into his arms, and they danced in the night.

The dance was broken by a knock on the door. It was brutal and insistent, the sound of approaching death. A stranger loomed at the threshold. He wore the chainmail of a French knight, but one who had deserted his own army to serve himself alone. Coldly, he turned to Farmer Raulin: 'You did not invite me to your feast, you peasant! Kneel at my feet and plead for mercy.' Yet the old man straightened his spine defiantly, his breath freezing in the chill of the night. He refused to yield.

The younger Raulin's blood exploded in rage, sickened at the insult to his father's honour. Drunk on his own courage, he swaggered up to the intruder. 'Get out of here – before I kick you out like a dog! This is my father's house; this hearth is ours. Begone!'

Silence hung there like an axe, suspended. The stranger grimaced. His was a cold and unyielding fury, as chilling as the northern rain. At last, he spoke, and his words lingered long after he had slipped away. 'Your life is forfeit, my child. Your account will be settled, and that soon enough.'

The stranger was gone. A raven screeched behind him in the night.

* * *

Long after midnight, an exuberant Raulin escorted his fiancée Jeanne and her family home to their farmstead. She wept with fear, shaking with dread, begging him to take Fidèle, her loyal dog, to guard him on his journey home. Yet Raulin felt fearless. He had faced boldly up to the oppressor this day and seen him off. Tonight he had become a man, and soon enough he would take his vows as a husband too, at the altar beneath the angels and the incense, in the church of the Holy Trinity. His road was hallowed now; every path would lead him home. He strode off into the night, her hound at his heels.

At a lonely crossroads, Fidèle abruptly stopped and let out a heartbreaking, terrified whine. For a moment the night was utterly silent, concealing its secrets. Then a band of horses clattered over the horizon. These were powerful steeds, bearing masked men, riding in force. In the moonlight, Raulin glimpsed flashes of heavy weaponry: swords, axes, battle shields. Instinctively, like a field-rat, he scurried into a ditch, willing himself to sink into its muddy, cold embrace.

The men passed. Then the sky cracked with a bolt of lightning. For a moment an electric white light burst over Jersey, flooding the fields like high noon. He ran, but there could be no escape now. He heard oaths, saw a blade slash at his brave dog. Then a mace was raised, and the back of his head was smashed like a snail's shell. Five burly men seized his limp body, binding his hands, throwing him onto the back of a horse like a stolen sheep.

* * *

Warmth filtered back first, just before the pain. Raulin was somewhere by the fireside again, dancing with his beloved. Then the sticky agony of his skull splintered the dream. He was indeed by a fire, but trapped somewhere in a dark cave, deep within a cliff, above a black beach.

The storm waters thundered and foamed outside; but in this den of thieves, all was merriment. The sheep-stealers feasted on legs of stolen mutton and downed jars of cider. Shadows flickered and danced on the walls. The brigands stuffed and gorged and belched. At last, they remembered their tethered victim, and they decided to hang him dead.

And then, as they tightened the rope around his neck, something unexpected happened. His beloved, beautiful Jeanne, ran into his arms.

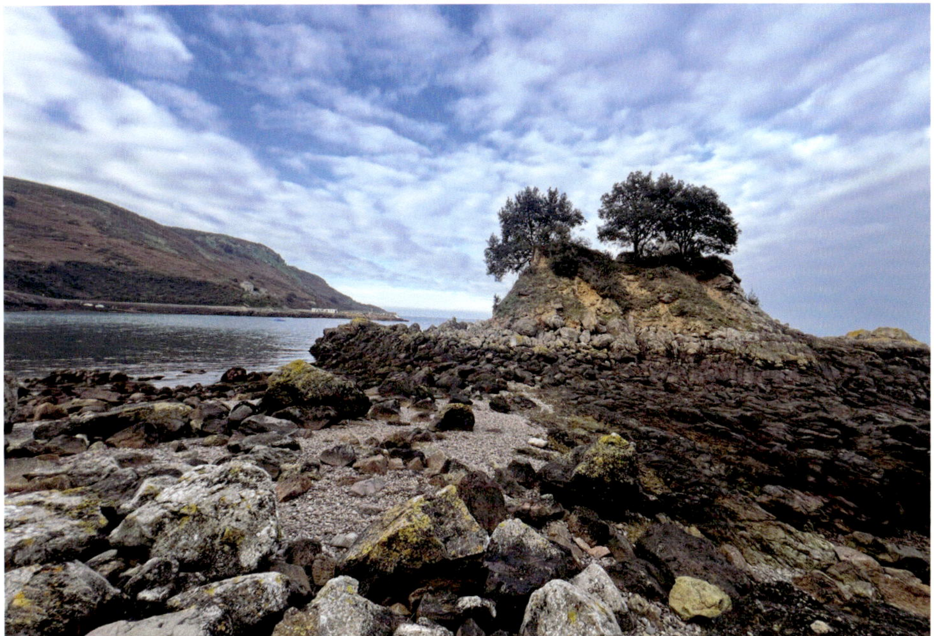

Bouley Bay in autumn. (Author)

* * *

Somehow, in the bitter hours of darkness, her whimpering, wounded dog had limped home. Fidèle's blood trail stained the dark country hedges. Woken by her bleeding, distressed hound, Jeanne had seized her courage and followed the trail to the foot of the cliff, down to the lair of the pirates. It was a fatal blunder. Now the robber chief sneered at his double prey. 'Behold these two little lambs, caught in a hunter's snare', he bellowed. 'Kill the boy; I will keep the girl for myself.'

In the darkness of the cave, armed men closed in. The gang surrounded them. Raulin, bound and wounded as he was, lurched forward to defend his beloved. There was a flash of steel in the darkness, and the first lamb was slain. Raulin bled to death on the rock-floor of the cave, his blood mingling with the rising waters. Then the pirate king closed in to seize Jeanne.

Too late, he realised she carried a concealed knife. With a primal shriek that could break the walls of the cave, Jeanne lunged straight at him. The blade broke clean in the chief's sternum, and he was dead before his corpse hit the floor.

Jeanne ran straight towards the open mouth of the cave. The surviving robbers were gaining on her, but she kept climbing over the treacherous rocks. The storm was screeching higher, and violent waves were plunging in from the north. Jeanne looked back at the welter of lights and men, the frenzy of knives and torches. Then a black wall of water broke over her, and she was flung straight into the maw of the sea.

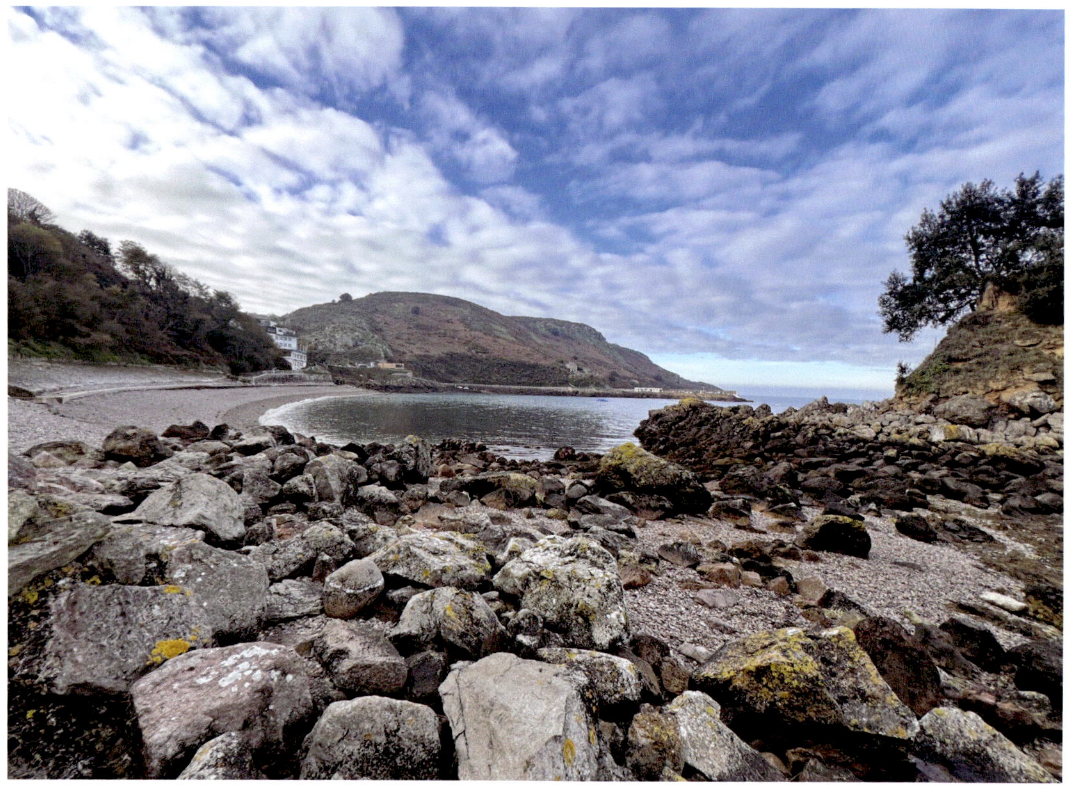

Rocks at Bouley Bay. (Author)

Her body was washed up days later on the October tides. The parishioners mourned and fasted; their fairest children were gone. Later that night, a funnel of carrion crows was seen rising from the base of the cliff. When the men of Trinity stumbled down into the empty cave, they found the wreckage of an abandoned feast. Two bodies lay on the cold stone floor: the pirate and his prey, broken in the shadows of the cave.

* * *

Today they call it *Le Creux de Bouanne*, and it is an accursed place. The north coast in these parts is a desolate shore. And when the tides roar in, and the waves shatter the high cliffs, they say that deep within the cave, you can still hear Jeanne wailing. The fishermen have an old name for this: *Les Cris des Tombelènes*.

We can hear her calling still, as the tides turn, as day becomes night, as the centuries scatter like pebbles on the seashore. She cries every night for her lost love, for a last glimpse of warmth and light, for everything that lies buried deep beneath the waves.

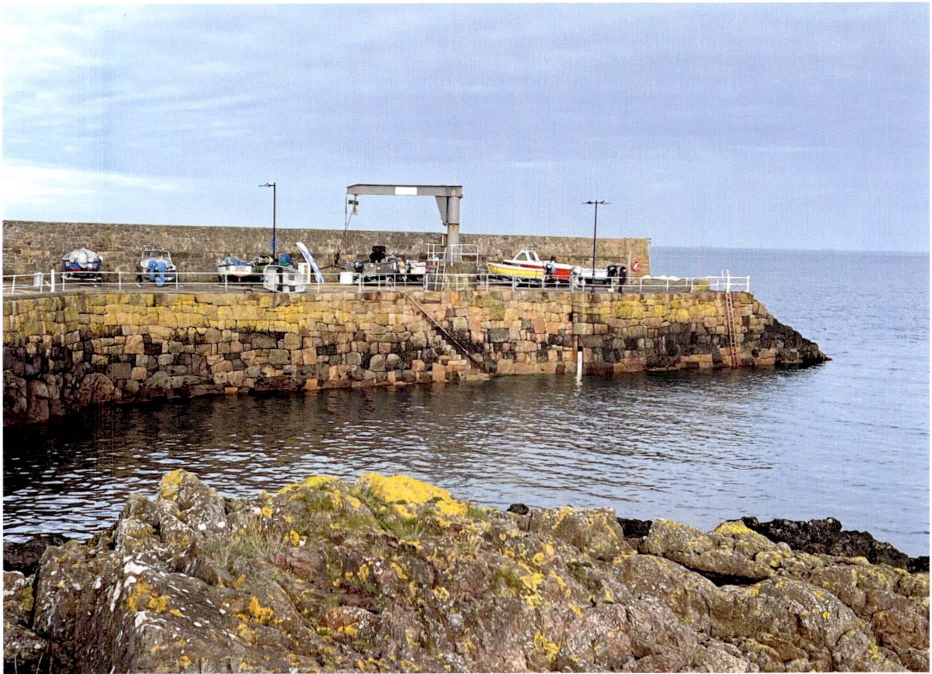

The pier at Bouley Bay. (Author)

The Storm Hound of Bouley
Trinity, Jersey, December 1629

At four o'clock, the light failed. A winter storm pummelled into Jersey, smiting the northern cliffs like a brawler's fist. A bolt of fire flared above the spire of Trinity church, striking it with the fury of a fiery angel. The lightning storm was over in moments, a flare of sheer white light, the gut-churning crash of falling masonry, and the reek of sulphur billowing above the village. Raindrops began to fall on Trinity like knives.

Michel, a farmer's son of seventeen, stepped straight out into the squall, herding his terrified cows into their flimsy barn, soothing their agitated cries with fresh hay. By the time he was done, the full frenzy of the storm had passed. Drenched but relieved, Michel watched as the lightning raced helter-skelter towards the southern horizon. The worst had passed, and a silky dusk settled upon the rain-lashed parish.

Yet Michel was suddenly troubled as he counted the necks of his small herd of cattle. One prime milk-cow was unaccounted for. He remembered the parable of the lost sheep he had often heard at Trinity church; how a farmer should go to the ends of the earth to save one of his own. This was not a matter of piety in his case, but simple financial necessity. Sighing, he set off into the night, crossing the black fields of his father's farm in search of the missing cow. Where might she have fallen?

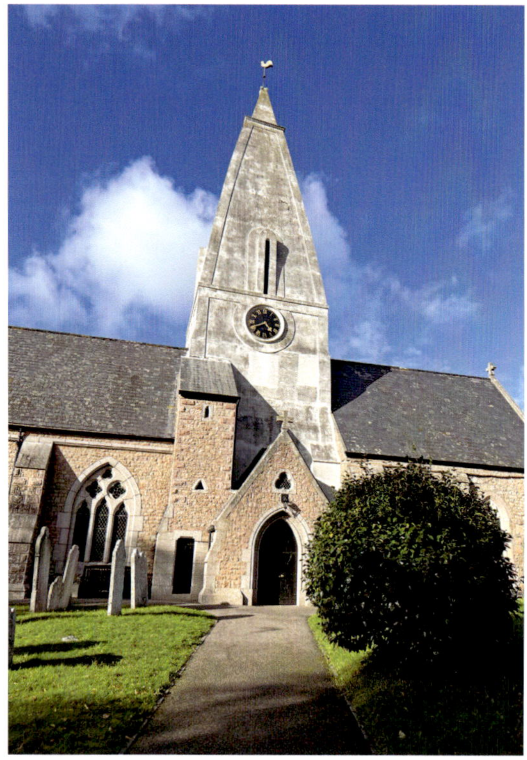

Trinity Church. (Author)

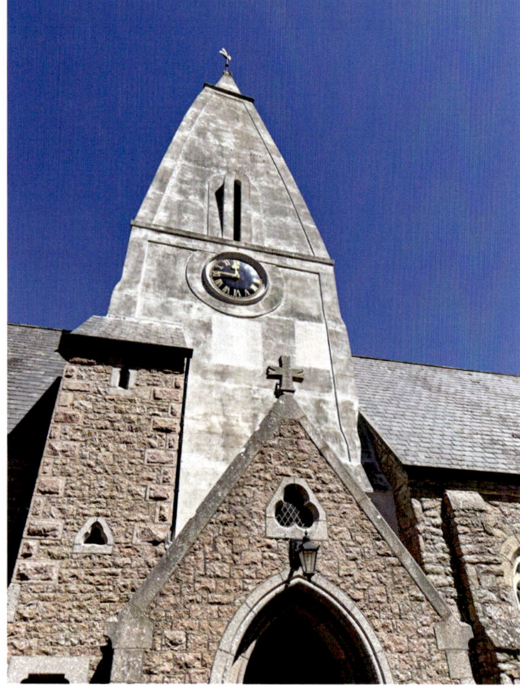

The tower of Trinity Church.
(Author)

The farmland soon petered out, and the wooded bay of Bouley lay beyond. It had no stone pier, of course, but was a safe anchorage for fishermen, a haven amidst the sheer cliffs of the rugged north. However, Michel disliked the coast; for one thing, he could not swim. An air of menace always seemed to hang over these parts like evening fog. There were swirling rumours of misbegotten happenings, of secrets best left untold.

Every little child whimpered at the tale of Lé Tchian du Bouôlay, the giant Black Dog of Bouley Bay that their grandmothers said stalked the beach. This was said to be the Storm Hound, the half-brother of Cerberus, plucked fresh from the gates of hell. They said he dragged before him a great iron chain that no mortal could grasp. His eyes were said to be blinding yellow saucers, and the mere sight of them turned strong legs to butter. This wolf feasted on the bones of men.

Michel scoffed at the fable, surely told to frighten errant children and scarcely credible even after a few jars of cider. After all, he knew these cliffs like the veins on his own body, or the tracks and dolmens that peppered his father's farmland. So, he strode boldly on into the watches of the night.

Eventually, he heard the lowing of his frightened cow, which must have fled right here, disorientated, lost in the storm. Michel advanced to the edge of the cliffs. These were amongst the highest vantage points in Jersey; the heavy mass of Sark loomed before him on the horizon, and the snaking arm of the French coast. Above it all, the gibbous moon hung like a lantern, and the sky billowed with night clouds.

Michel was closing in on his missing cow. Taking the secret paths to the shoreline, descending rapidly as the cliffs fell away into the sea, he made good progress. The cries grew nearer, and he saw her, frozen on a rocky ledge overlooking the moonlit bay. She was clearly too terrified to take another step, for fear of plummeting to the beach hundreds of feet below. Michel coaxed her forward, and her soft warm muzzle reached into his hand. It was midnight, but at last he had found his prize.

A cloud snuffed out the moon, and in an instant his joy froze to fear, as if the tide had suddenly drained from Bouley Bay. He heard the blunt, remorseless clanking of an iron chain. Far too loud to be an illusion; this was the unmistakable ring of steel striking rock on the beach below. Now it was advancing towards his shelter in the wooded glade. A terrifying flash of yellow glinted before him in the trees. They seemed like the baleful saucer eyes of something unearthly, bent on his blood.

Michel reeled as if drunk, poleaxed by the mounting terror in his own mind. The saucer eyes approached. At last, the deep-chested baying of a great dog filled the forest, the roar of a hound that was poised to strike. Michel slumped to his knees in the dead of the Trinity night, his face on the ground, choking with fear. The violent blow to his head that sent him into darkness fell as gently as a blessing.

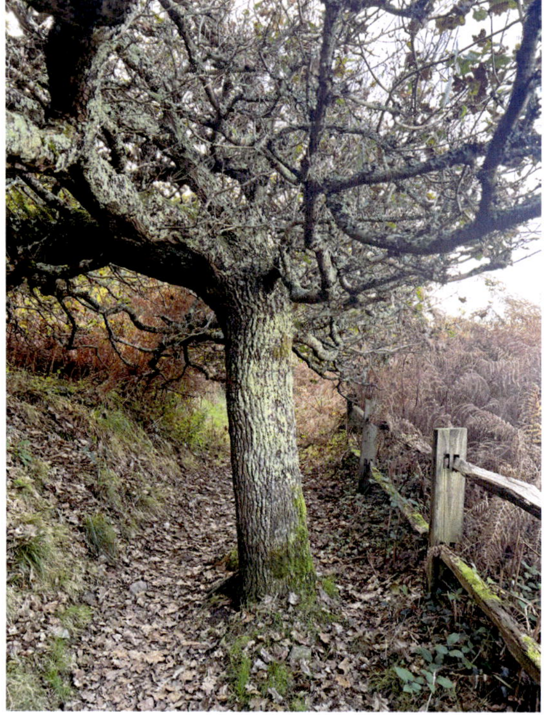

Tree at Bouley Bay. (Author)

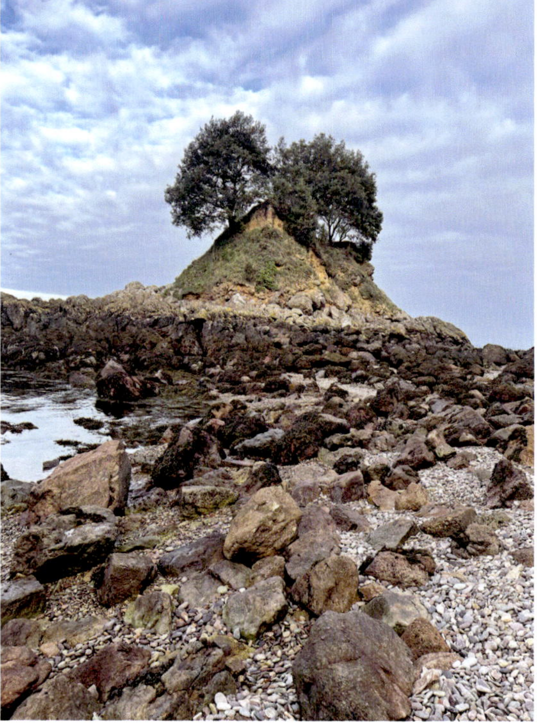

Trees on the tidal island at Bouley
Bay. (Author)

In the event the encounter did not unduly delay the evening's delivery, for the smugglers had almost completed their sweaty task of hauling the barrels along the chain up the steep cliff. Jersey's cellars were stuffed full of the finest illicit brandy that night, and their own purses bulged with silver coin.

The smugglers snuffed out their yellow circular lanterns that served as eyes and led their pet bloodhound back to their pinnace. Along the way home they stumbled across a lost cow, and they brutally slaughtered it, to serve as a chilling warning to the locals. Then their boat glided away into the night, as if they had never been there. Bouley Bay settled back into the sad sleep of winter.

* * *

Young Michel was found near the shoreline the next morning, shivering and delirious, ranting incoherently. They warmed him by the fireside, and he would be well enough in time. Yet thereafter he would become a brooding, silent man, with a terrible fear of the cliffs and a superstitious, insatiable belief in the Black Dog of Bouley Bay.

To be fair, the facts of the incident spoke for themselves. The Constable of Trinity addressed the parish the next day, detailing the tell-tale evidence: the chain-link imprinted in the soft mud of the road, the hallmark of the storm hound. Young Michel must have been lucky to survive, he observed. After all, he was found near the body of his own dead cow, whose belly had been slashed open, presumably by a savage beast.

In the light of these disturbing events, it was only right and proper that a strict curfew should be observed, and parishioners should avoid the coast at night. The Constable solemnly prayed for the safety of his parish, beseeching them to be protected until the shadow of the Dog had passed.

Then he retreated homeward, to enjoy a glass of fresh French brandy.

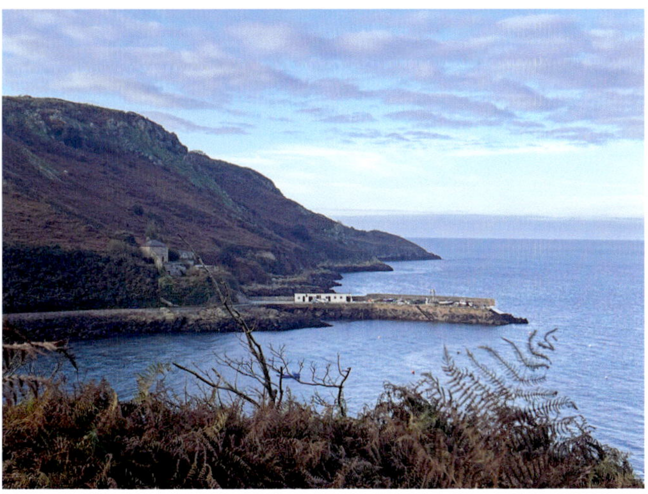

Bouley Bay and its pier.
(Author)

Tales of Town

St Helier, Jersey's only town, is rich in mystery and legend. At its heart lies Royal Square, dominated by a statue of King George II in the robes of a Roman Emperor. On 6 January 1781, bullets flew all around it, as the Battle of Jersey unfolded. That fateful day, the invading French army of Baron de Rullecourt was repelled, and the Island was saved. De Rullecourt himself died in the firefight, along with Major Peirson, the brave Yorkshireman who managed to foil his plans. Both are buried in the nearby town church of Saint Helier.

The church's red granite walls have borne witness to many turbulent centuries, including the dark days of the Occupation. Yet its story – and that of the town that bears its name – dates from a much older age. This is the tale of Helier the man, a holy wanderer from afar who settled on this distant shore. His own Hermitage, a rocky outcrop in St Aubin's Bay, is still a place of pilgrimage. It is now joined by a breakwater to Elizabeth Castle and is a popular tourist destination. On this rock, long ago, the saint lived, worked and prayed. Until one day, the dark clouds on the horizon – ever after known as *les vailes dé St Hélyi*, or the sails of St Helier – swooped in to claim his life.

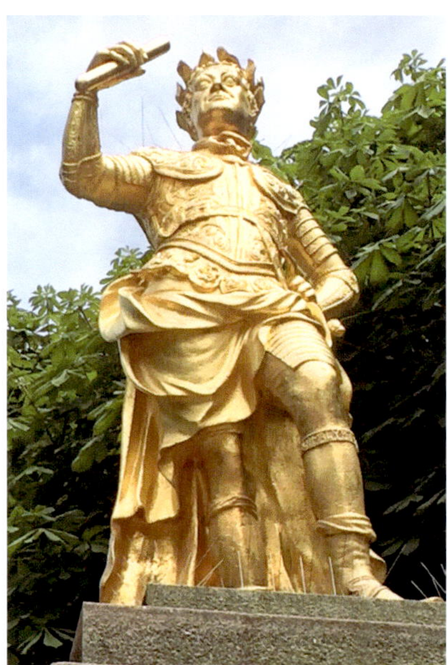

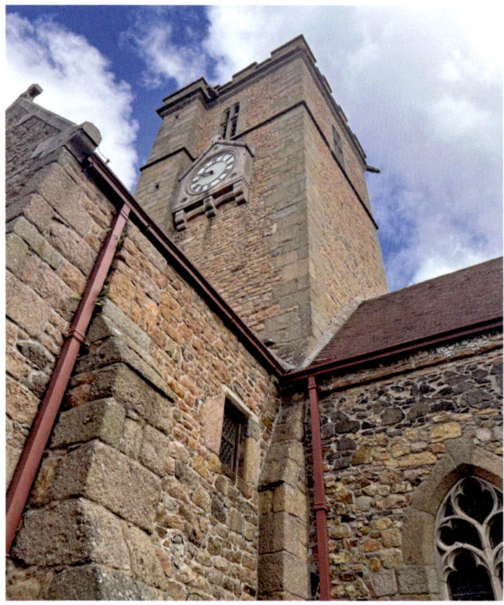

Above left: Statue of King George II in Royal Square. (Author)

Above right: St Helier Town Church. (Author)

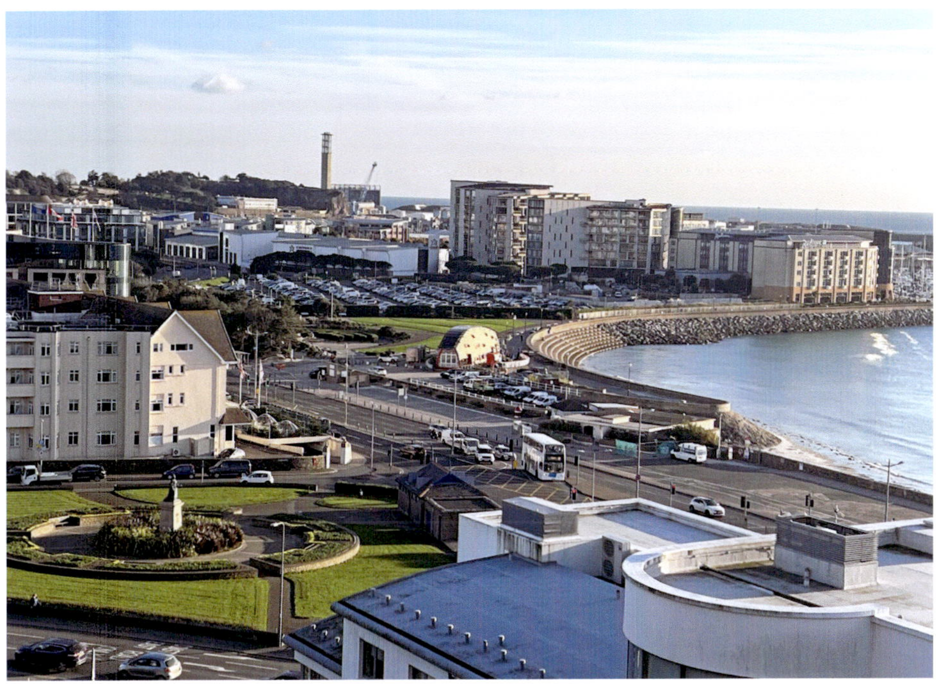

View of St Helier Waterfront. (Author)

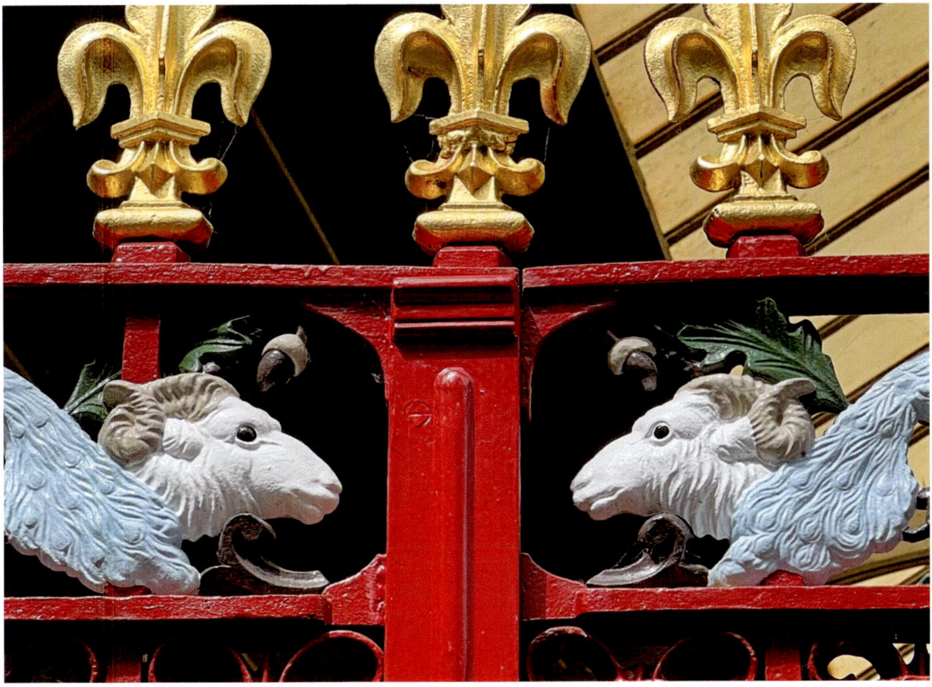

Detail from the Central Market in St Helier. (Author)

The Sails of Saint Helier

A Jersey Fisherman, AD 555

Helier first found us clinging to the sands, vulnerable and afraid. We fisherfolk crouched in our marshes by the shore, marvelling at this stranger who had sought us out. He was dressed in a simple robe and carried no coin. The seas around Jersey were infested with pirates, and yet he held no sword.

Few came this way, except to plunder. Helier had no earthly goods, yet we learned that he was the son of a wealthy nobleman. He had relinquished it all to roam the world as a pilgrim saint. What, he marvelled, did it profit a man to gain the whole world, yet lose his soul?

Helier hailed from the continent beyond, from the vast disc of cities and spires and castles and palaces that we glimpse on the horizon. He was born to the governor of a teeming city called Tongeren, a Roman frontier town. Fleeing his gilded prison, he wandered for months in the forests and deserts, calling to God, seeking his flock.

We know so little of the world beyond these shores. Our forefathers told stories of the great Empire that had come and gone, leaving us in a valley of shadows. They told tales of great ships and legions, of temples and palaces, of the glory of the time before the fall. Occasionally we glimpsed the beauty of what once had been: a stunning fragment of blue mosaic, or a dead Emperor's face on a fading coin.

On summer mornings, we caught conger eels in the great bay and hung them out to dry on the sands. When they were cured, we feasted. We climbed the hills to watch for raiding parties. Whenever the longships drew in, we fled like ghosts to our sanctuaries in the deep heart of the Island. Our straw huts would burn, but we would survive. Such was the endless cycle of life, of suffering and enduring, winter and summer.

Then Helier shared a new Gospel.

* * *

At first, we mocked the newcomer, threatening him with oaths and curses. Yet he stepped forward, not to greet our leaders or strongmen, but to embrace poor old Antequil, the beggar who infirmity and age had left broken on the sands. Helier looked him in the eye and commanded him to rise. We watched thunderstruck as a miracle unfolded before our eyes. Antequil skipped like a lamb to meet us, a young man once more.

The whole village believed. And that same day we built a church to mark the hour. Helier's disciple Romard preached diligently, but the great man himself was an enigma, a shadow-priest who was rarely seen. He lived as a hermit on the rock in the bay, sleeping on a bed of stone, driven into delirium by sunlight and saltwater. When the Saxon raiders drew near, he would light a flame in the hollow, as a secret signal for us to head to the hills.

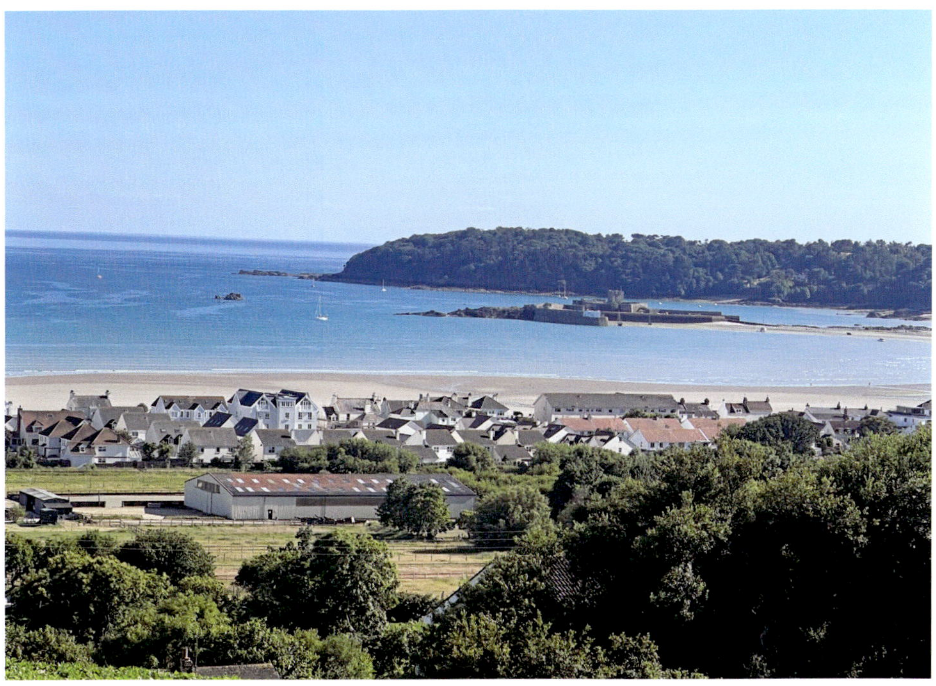

St Aubin's Bay. (Author)

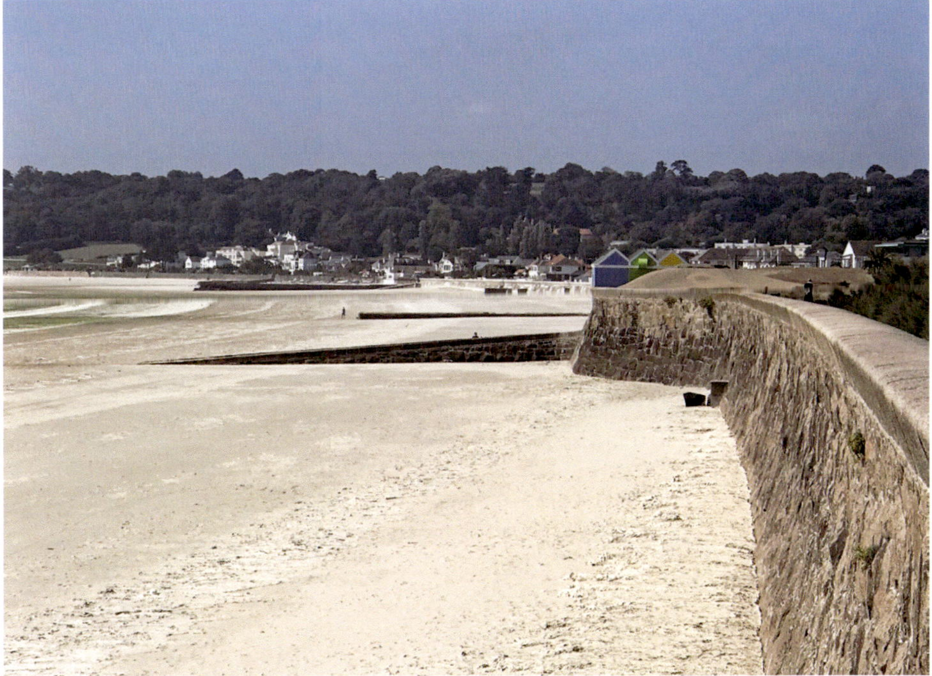

The sands of St Aubin's Bay. (Author)

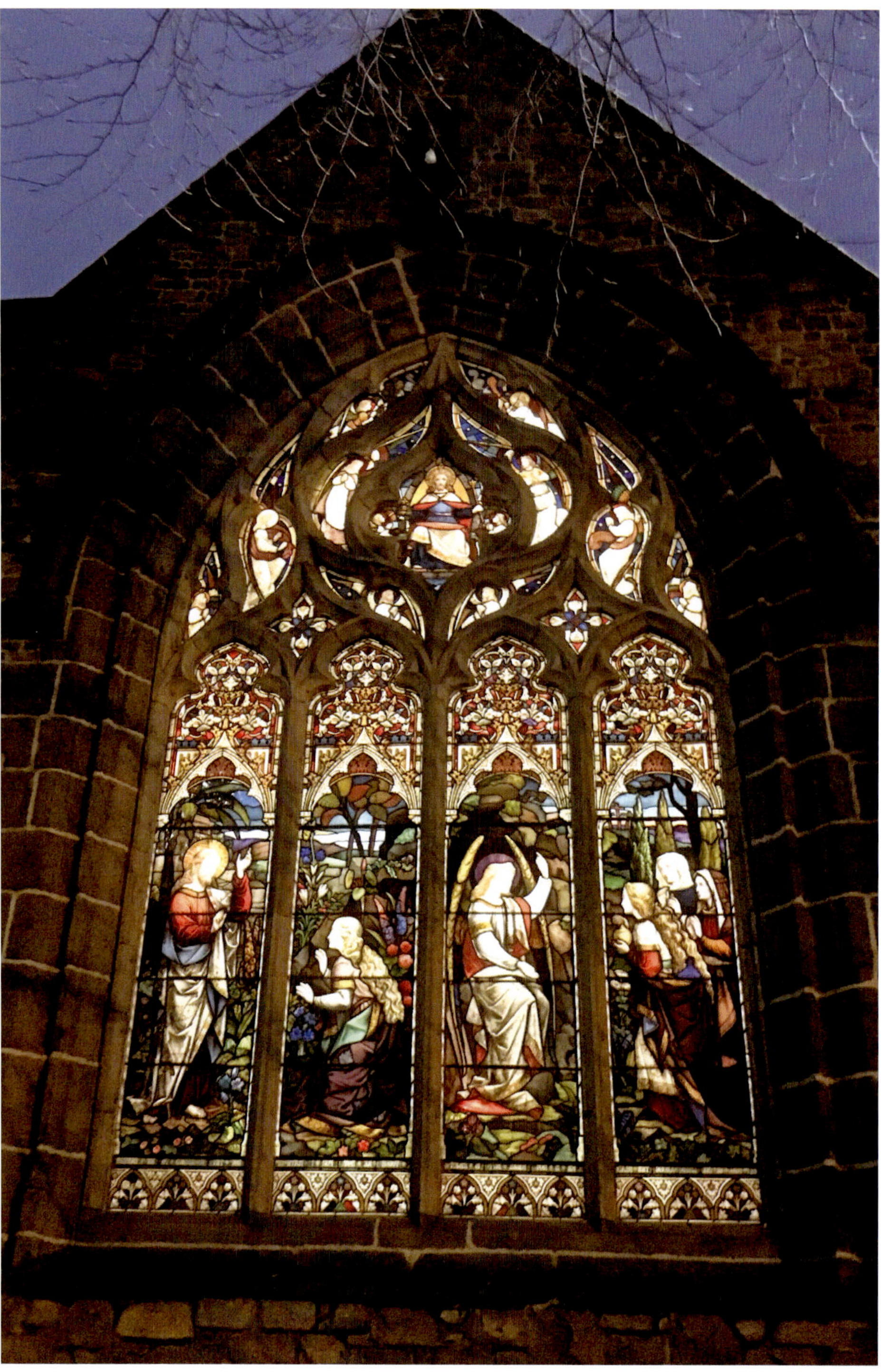

St Helier Parish Church – the Town Church. (Author)

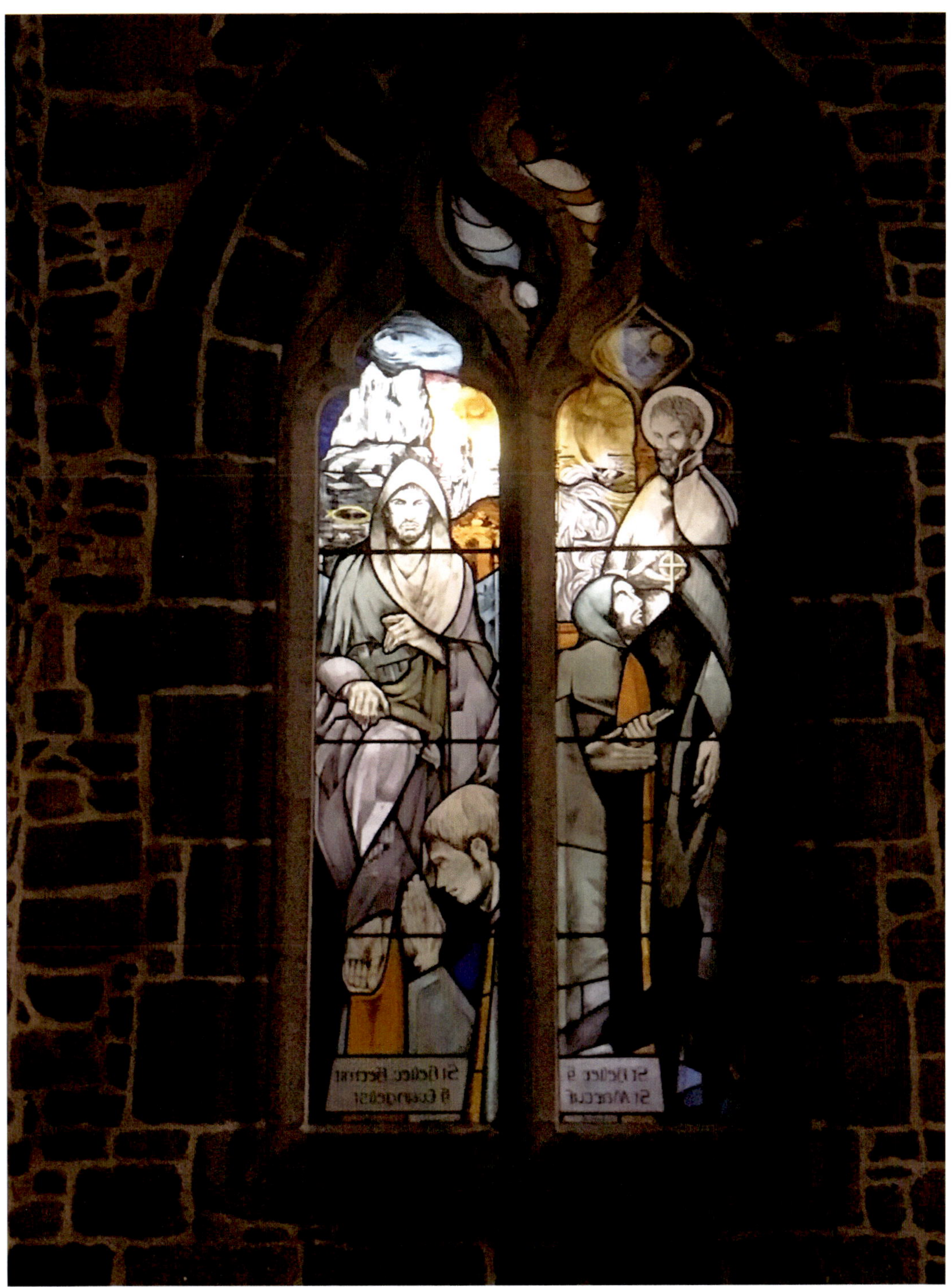

St Helier window in the Town Church. (Author)

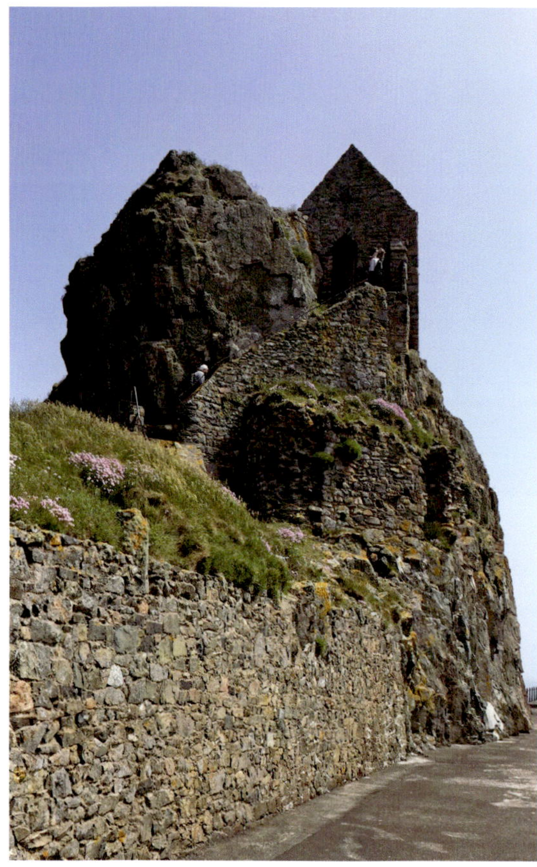

The Hermitage of St Helier.
(Author)

Helier left this earth in the year of our Lord 555, on one of the longest days of summer, when the heavy sun simmers like a fireball over the bay. He spied a dark fist of cloud, incongruous on such a spotless, glittering day. *That is no cloud: it is a sail!*

The frail saint, his body weakened by weeks of fasting, struggles to light the flame. But he perseveres, and soon trails of dark smoke twist into the golden skies. The townsfolk heed the warning, grab their children and their hens and melt into the valleys. Not a hair on their heads will be harmed.

It is too late for me. I am fishing by the creek and there is no time to flee. I can only crawl into the shadow of a red granite rock, and watch the story unfurl before me like a tapestry. The raiders are closing in now – a fleet of Saxon longships, bristling with spears and shields, blazing with the pennants of war. Heavily armoured warriors sent from the North, hell-bent on mayhem and plunder.

Helier calmly rises to meet them, his right hand clutching a fragment of the Gospel, his left hand raised in blessing. The raiders spit and jeer at the old fool. He is scarcely worth the physical effort of a strike.

The Saxon captain steps forward, draped in full chain-mail armour. He roars with mockery and raises his meaty arms to the sky. The frail hermit outstretches his hands, for he is already seeing angels ascending and descending on the Son of Man.

Twin axe blades flash in the summer sun. I see a man fall to the rock, as lightly as a seagull's feather.

I cannot explain the next few moments. Heaven invades earth. I watch in awe as a radiant saint, bursting with light, seems to carry his own severed head back to the shore.

The Saxon murderers are falling to their knees in dread, beating their chests and begging for their lives. They stagger back to their boats and cast off in disarray, scuttling off over the horizon, whimpering. Then the shining figure melts into the setting sun.

* * *

The next morning, I tiptoe out to Helier's rock, to the scene of the miracle, but my friend is gone. There is only an empty stone bed, a broken axe blade, and a sense of grace departed. I whisper a prayer and leave my friend's memory to the safekeeping of the rock, the crying of the gulls, and the mercy of the tides.

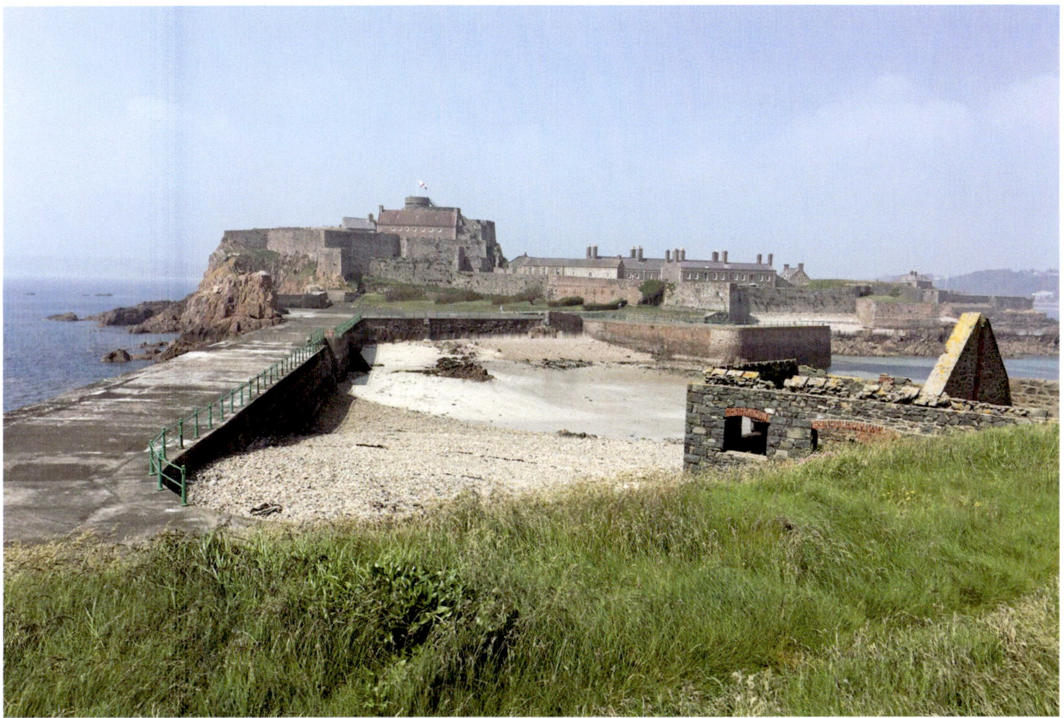

View of Elizabeth Castle from Saint Helier's Hermitage. (Author)

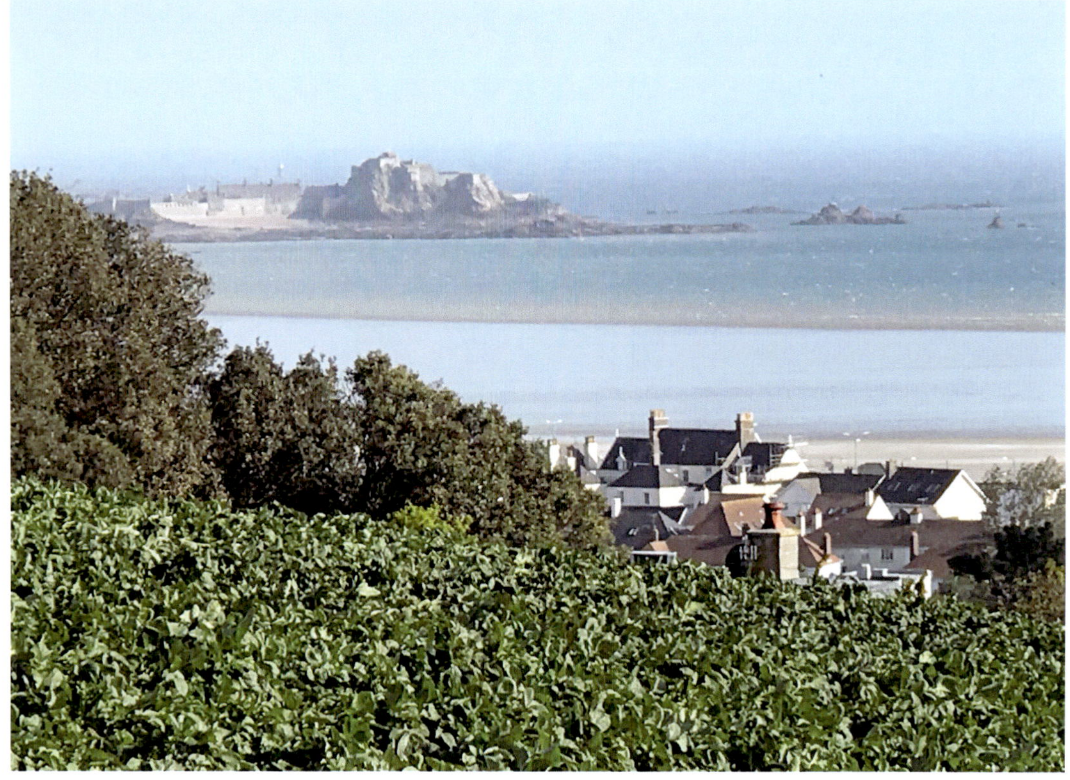

A view of Elizabeth Castle. (Author)

The Lost Stones of Jersey

In the centuries after St Helier, the cluster of fishermen's huts named after him expanded into a little town. After the Battle of Jersey in 1781 that saved the Island from French invasion, the British Government set about strengthening the Island's defences. The decision was taken to fortify the Town Hill, Mont de la Ville, and turn it into a fortification – Fort Regent. The decision would not come without cost.

***

Jersey's Stonehenge, they called it, a ring of stones that must have endured thousands of winters and glimmered through countless summers. The wheel of history turned, empires rose and fell, and the blunt molars on the hill outlasted them all. The dolmen and their passage grave remained on the barren outcrop above St Helier, until they too were buried by time and age.

The Town Hill was a sacred place. When mysterious footprints were discovered, believed to be those of the Virgin Mary, the chapel of Notre Dame de Pas was built in her honour on its south-eastern flank. The hill was a powerful

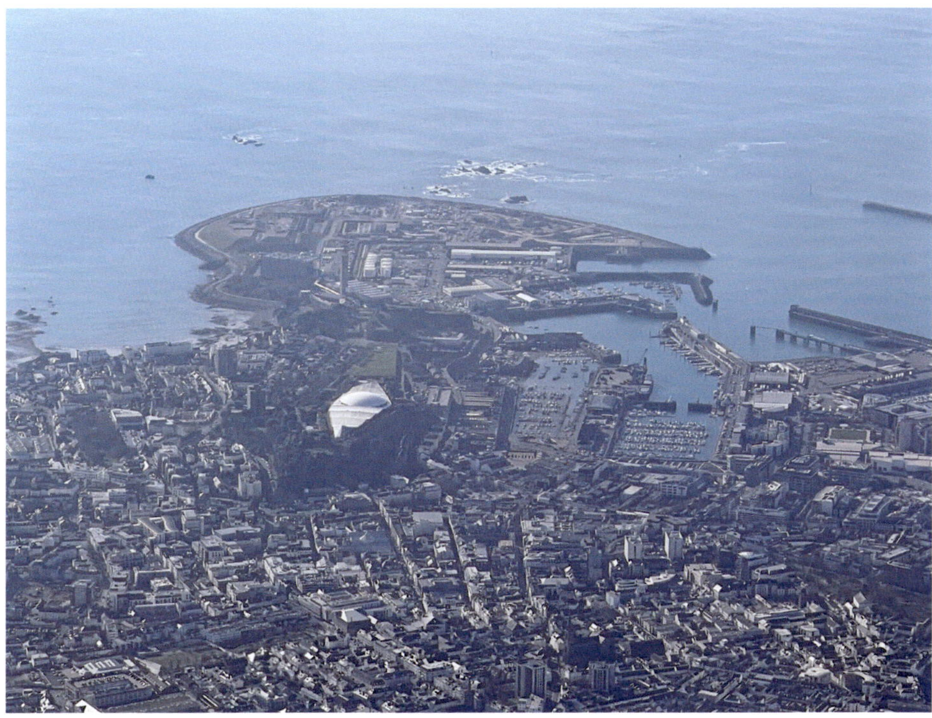

Aerial view of St Helier. (Author)

vantage point, towering over the straggling huts of St Helier that gathered at its feet. In times of peace, the Seigneur of Samarès chased rabbits over its summit, and cattle grazed idly upon its bleak slopes. In times of war, its commanding views became a vital strategic asset.

The recent French invasion – when the Battle of Jersey raged savagely in Royal Square – revealed the sheer inadequacy of Jersey's defences. The time had finally come to tame the Town Hill and remodel it in the service of war. It would become Jersey's Rock of Gibraltar, a stout stronghold, a British fortress. The Governor of Jersey, General Henry Seymour Conway, gave orders to scour the land, mapping it and moulding it, making plans for the work to come.

We meet him on a humid August morning in 1785, as sea-fog is rolling in from the south. The Colonel of the Militia is adamant; the drill field must be cleared today. His men would rather be downing cider in the taverns, but today they must level the land. They set to work with picks and shovels, sweat soon rising beneath their red militia jackets.

When the men start to break up a grassy mound, they strike hard rock. To their astonishment, this hillock is perched on granite stones, and they do not seem to have fallen here naturally. These sentinels have been painstakingly arranged; guardians left by a race of ancient men. A dark corridor opens into the earth, a passage grave leading into the darkness of a forgotten world.

The militiamen shrug. Mysterious barrows have long been part of the warp and weft of Jersey's landscape, after all. Granite teeth glint across every parish; broken ceremonial stones have littered the hills since time immemorial. These new discoveries are mere obstacles to an evening of good cheer and ale. Yet suddenly a shiver runs through the camp; the Governor himself is approaching. The militiamen hastily smarten themselves, and assemble, and salute.

General Conway, an Old Etonian and self-appointed scion of the Enlightenment, sweeps into the field. He is utterly bewitched by the discovery. He peers into the darkness, running his hand over the cold stone that has been buried for so long. His antiquarian enthusiasms piqued, the General demands further and deeper excavations. The soldiers return to their labours.

And here they will unearth a perfect Stonehenge in miniature, a stone circle, the inheritance of a mysterious and inaccessible age. The crowning glory of Jersey's Neolithic past was revealed. Standing in a 72-foot circle, the granite monoliths were finally exposed to the fresh sunlight of an utterly different world.

Conway exulted in the discovery. It must be a Druid's temple, he mused, a historically valuable relic of the wild time before the Romans subdued the world. The wily landowners of La Vingtaine shrugged at the General's curiosity, his eccentric interest in a bundle of old stones. Yet they quickly spied a way to inveigle their way into his good favour. They would proffer him the stones as a gift of thanksgiving.

They beseeched him 'to be so good as to accept the ancient monument which has been recently discovered on La Montagne de la Ville. They trust that His

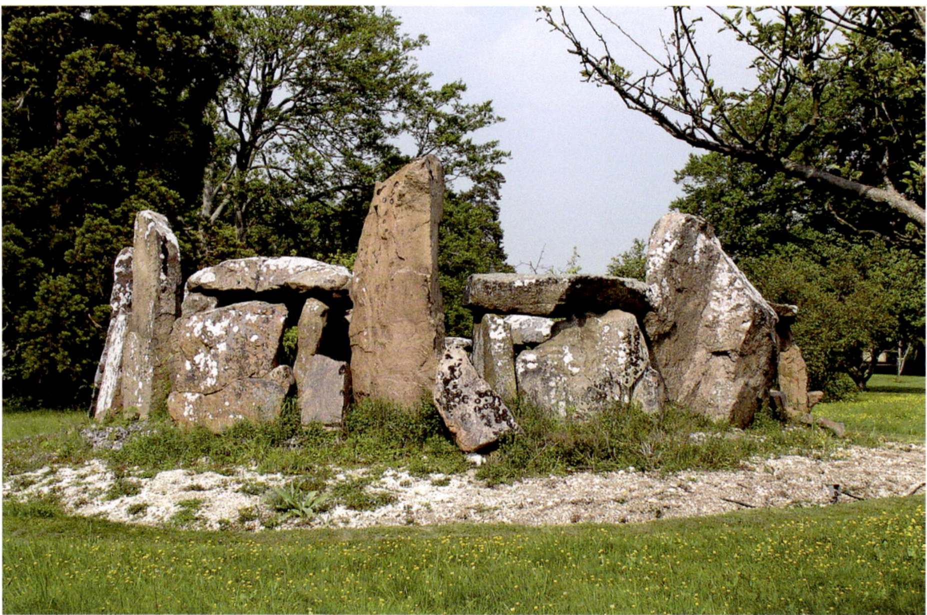

Le Mont de la Ville. (Courtesy of www.prehistoricjersey.net)

Excellency will not decline to accept this feeble but sincere tribute of their gratefulness.' Legend has it that Conway was initially reluctant, fearing the cost of transit, but Horace Walpole, son of the first British Prime Minister, urged him to receive the gift. 'Pray do not disappoint me but transport the Cathedral of your island to your domain on our continent.'

Conway yielded, for the pile of rocks would make a most charming addition to his English country estate at Park Place. So, in 1788, the stones were felled from their hilltop, hauled onto ships, and they crossed the rough seas to a new island. Their old home was already dying, for in the decades to come, the Town Hill would be transformed into a mighty fortress. It would be given a new name, too: Fort Regent.

The old Town Hill was gone, fortified by the might of the British Army. The medieval Chapel of Notre Dame de Pas was blown up in 1814, its historic stones shredded, lest they provide shelter for an invading force. In time the Fort itself would become a relic, and was crowned by a graceful, mighty dome, until that too fell into a time of decay.

The circle, however, endured. Near the banks of the meandering Thames, the dolmen was reassembled and embellished. The red granite stones that once towered over the tides of Jersey, and the drowned coast of St Clement, found a strange afterlife in the gentle folds of an Oxfordshire country estate.

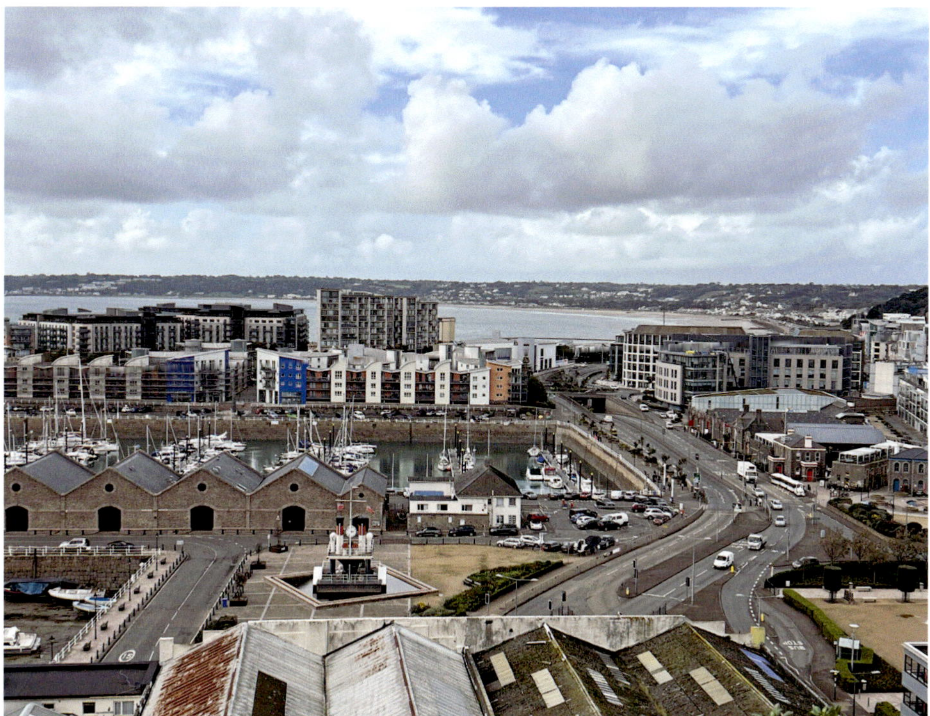

The view from Fort Regent today. (Author)

The stones stand there to this day, lost fragments of Jersey; a scattering of wild red granite nestled in an English country garden. The sea still sings in their landlocked veins.

The centuries have slipped by like sand. The stones wait in silence, far from the barren hill, far from the place they knew before. Some say they will find their way home in time, and the lost stones of Jersey will return.

The Doomed Ship: A Channel Tragedy

The loss of Jersey's standing stones to England proved to be a harbinger of things to come. The Island had long been a haven for continental radicals and revolutionaries. Victor Hugo found sanctuary here for three years, before settling in Guernsey. Karl Marx himself holidayed in St Helier.

Yet in Victorian times, St Helier rapidly anglicised, with the English language definitively replacing both Jèrriais and French as the talk of the town. Jersey thrived as a retirement home for Imperial functionaries, and as a balmy tourist destination far from the smog and soot of metropolitan Britain. The daily steamships from Southampton to St Helier ran as smooth as clockwork, until, in the dying years of Queen Victoria's reign, one of them foundered. This is her story.

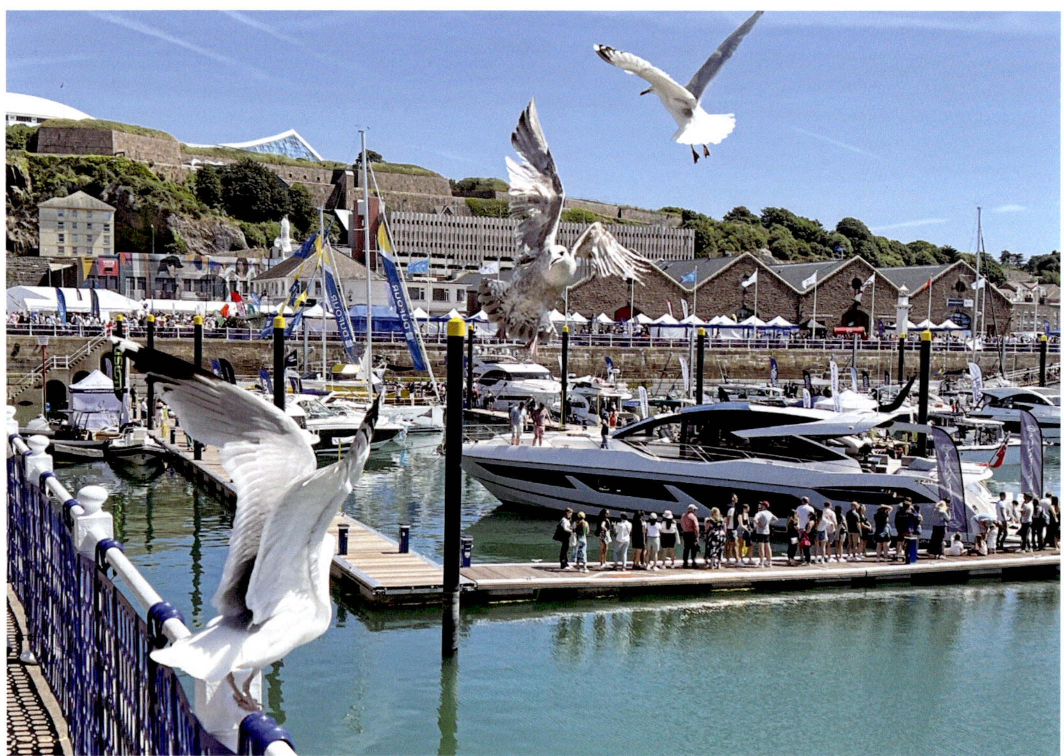

St Helier Harbour during the Boat Show. (Author)

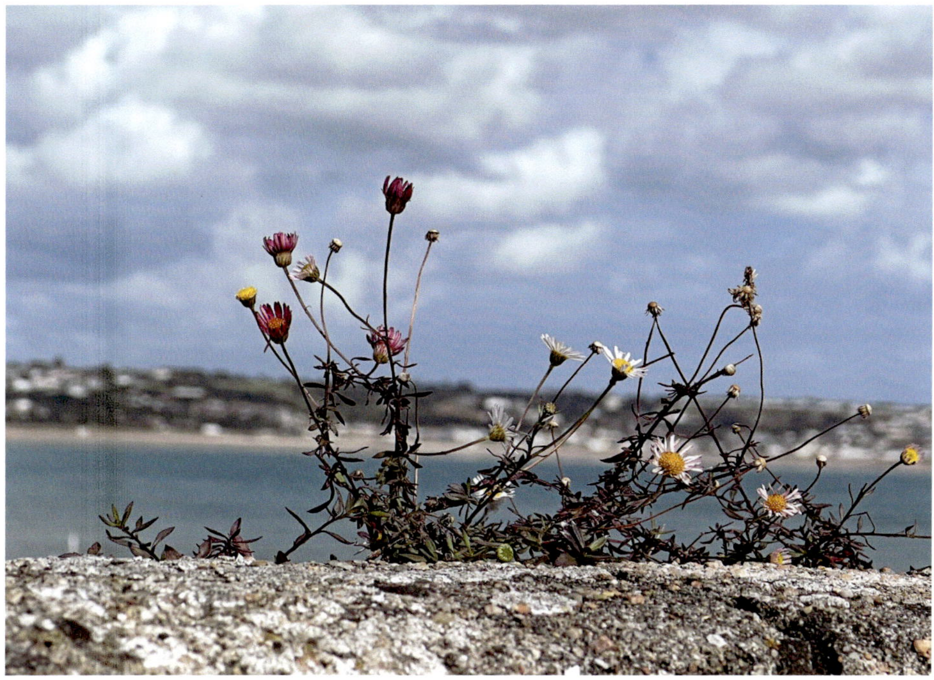

Flowers at St Aubin's Fort. (Author)

SS *Stella*, 30 March 1899, The Casquets, near Alderney

March proved deathly icy, a month of buds freezing on the branches, in a year without a spring. In America, freak snowstorms smothered the South, with snowball fights on the steps of the Florida statehouse. Britain's fate was less exotic, with rain-drenched gloom and vicious frosts that strangled the first daffodils.

Yet the Easter holidays were coming. Colonel George Dixon, of Surrey, longed for the succour of milder climes, and booked a family holiday. A Channel Islands break was always an alluring prospect; to step from the train at Southampton and stroll to the quay was sheer ease. That March morning, 200 passengers stepped on board the magnificent SS *Stella*, and its state-of-the-art electric lighting glinted invitingly in the morning light.

It was the first cruise of the holiday season. Captain Reeks knew that the SS *Ibex*, his bitter rival, would be hard on his heels. The last ship to arrive in the islands would be forced to wait its turn to dock at St Helier. The race was on. In this battle of wills, *Stella* was a name to conjure with; her powerful triple-expansion engines and a racing speed of 18 knots gave her a powerful advantage.

At 11.20 a.m. on Maundy Thursday, the *Stella* slipped out of port. The sun was glittering on the waves; it was shaping up to be a smooth crossing. The hours slid by. Captain Reeks knew the Casquet rocks lay on his course, but heaven knew they were paper tigers these days, defanged by a great foghorn that roared three great blasts with clockwork precision. And this afternoon, as the *Stella* suddenly pierced a cotton wool mountain of sea-mist, he heard no such warning.

The Channel weather had turned on a penny. A veil of freezing fog descended, white and cold. The chill insinuated every cloak, and the wind whipped every shawl. Colonel Dixon, on deck, thought he heard a faint sound from afar, but it was hard to discern when the wind made every ear sing. Instead, he turned to an officer. 'It is unfortunate, this fog coming on.' 'Yes, it has spoiled a good run,' the sailor replied. An elderly passenger muttered that he had never seen such speed in these conditions before. SS *Stella* plunged heedlessly on into the fog.

Visibility dropped like a stone. The crockery in the first-class lounge was shaking, vibrating with the extreme speed. Dark-liveried servants secured it in place, and then the urgent clattering eased. And there was just the eerie silence again, of water parting at the rate of knots, of the white haze all around, and the icy breath of the sea.

The clock struck four, and the world ended. The angels announced this with three trumpet blasts that physically shook the ship and left the sailors clutching their ears. The din was coming from directly above; SS *Stella* was at the very foot of the foghorn. Colonel Dixon gasped, but the reflex of his military training swiftly asserted itself and he appraised the situation. A vicious rock, taller than the ship itself, loomed just yards ahead of them.

The ship screeched into full speed astern, lurching violently, felling the legs of men like trees. Then the body of the ship was ripped open like the belly of a hare. Colonel Dixon felt the ship slice away beneath him, as a granite ridge amputated the hull. He whispered an urgent prayer.

* * *

SS *Stella* would be granted no languorous, gradual slide into the oblivion; no bands would play on deck as gentlemen exchanged farewells over choice brandy. The razor reefs of the Channel Islands inflicted a swifter death. Within seven minutes of impact, the ship would be swallowed by the freezing sea.

The crew, with commendable precision, started to lower the lifeboats. Their discipline was astonishing, for the deck was already the angle of a sloping roof. Mary Ann Rogers, the chief stewardess, saw most of the women and children to safety in a boat. She sacrificed her own lifejacket for a young girl. Some urged her to jump to safety, but the lifeboat lay low in the water and was clearly overladen; she would not risk the lives of her passengers. She waved a cheery 'Good-bye' and continued to do her duty.

Colonel Dixon, meanwhile, scrambled with his wife and children into the starboard lifeboat. Four boats were safely down; a fifth set to launch. The deck was bucking high now, reaching a tipping point. Then the waters surged in, and the boilers exploded. A series of terrifying thuds ensued, with a ferocious hiss of steam and a stinging mist that covered everything. In the chaos, the fifth lifeboat capsized during launch, spewing women and children into the icy maw of the sea.

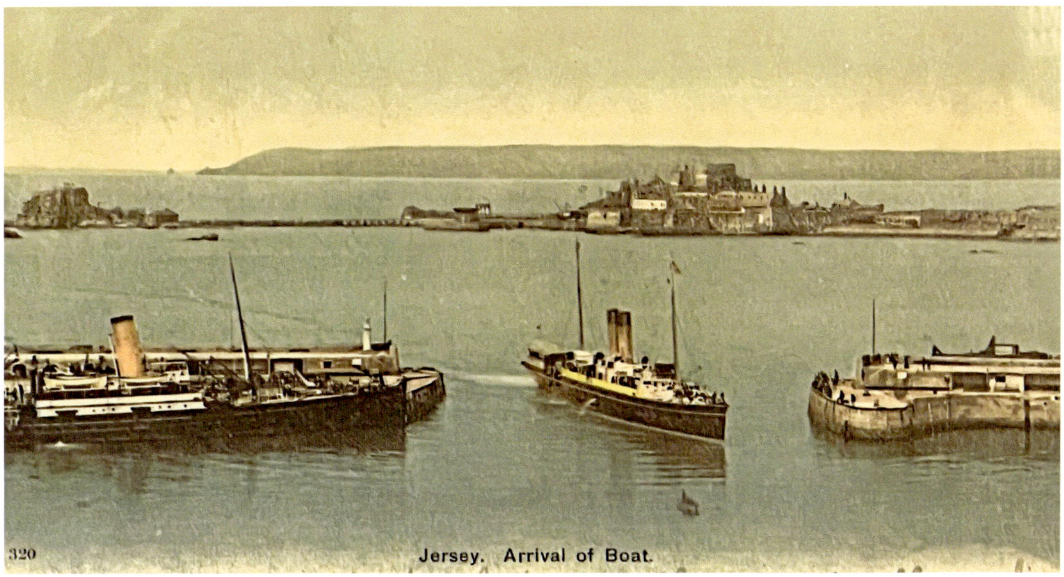

Jersey – arrival of the boat. Postcard from the reign of King Edward VII (1901–10).

The ship was almost vertical now, readying for its fatal dive. A young mother and her two sons floundered on the deck. The youngest was clutching his cherished football. In her last desperate moments, she tied him to his football for buoyancy, just before the ship started the final plunge.

The four lifeboats pushed out into the frigid water, and the survivors watched the tragedy unfold like a tableau from a horrific Bosch etching. Mary Ann Rogers was heard to cry 'Lord, have me!' as she tumbled into the abyss. Someone grabbed the young lad with the football and dragged him safely into a skiff. He would live, but never see his mother or brother again.

Driving a terrifying vortex in its wake, the SS *Stella* plunged down to the seabed. Men floundered like seals in the water, gasping and screaming. Thirty people clung desperately to the roof of a large furniture van, which was floating away, and others swam for the rocks. Captain Reeks himself had gone down with his ship, and a hundred more would be dead by nightfall.

On the starboard lifeboat, a man was hanging on the back of the boat, shivering and spluttering. He hooked his arm in, and it felt as icy as a corpse. He heard voices calling for him to be thrown back in the water, like a fish; best not to rock the boat. Yet one burly man dissented and manhandled the man to safety. He spluttered on the boards of the boat like an eel. A lady wrapped him in her cloak and slowly he was coaxed back to warmth and life. The voices that a moment earlier had called for him to drown were shamed and stilled.

The foghorn keepers above, snug in their lighthouse, never once realised that anything at all was amiss. They slumbered right through the unspeakable tragedy, as men froze to death on the rocks below them.

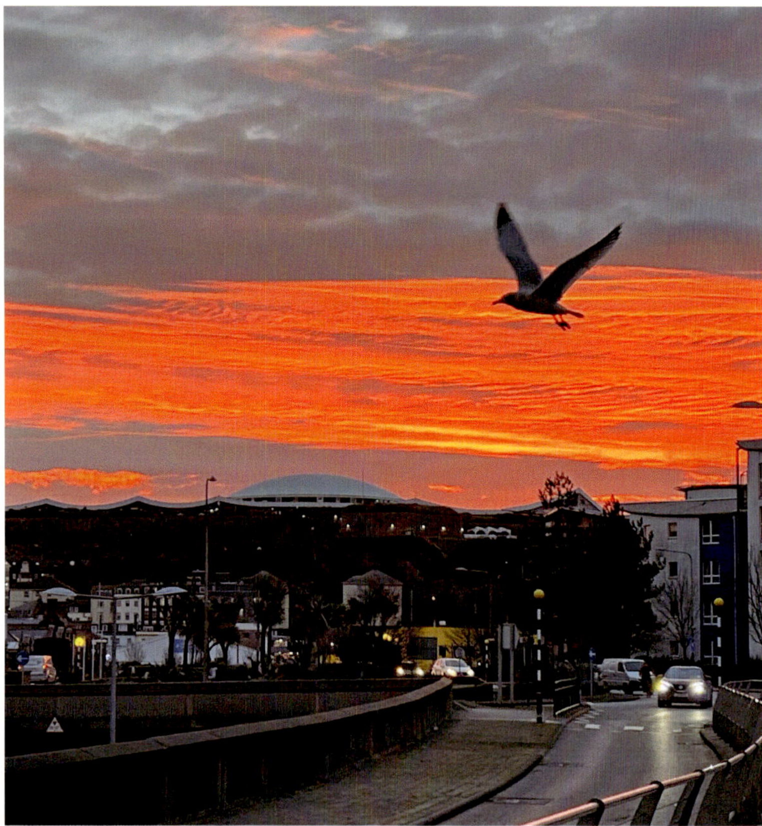

A winter's sunrise
with Fort Regent
on the horizon.
(Author)

* * *

It was the early hours of Good Friday. Back in Southampton, a troubled and angry crowd was gathering in the street outside the LSWR offices. The SS *Stella* had not made expected landfall and its position was unknown. Then a telegram arrived from Guernsey, with the dreaded words: STELLA HAS GONE DOWN.

The passengers in the boats had paddled desperately, seeking to keep off the evil rocks. The little lifeboats were swept almost to the French coast, but as the tide turned, they were flung back towards the rocks. Horrifically, there were men still clinging on there, half-dead after the lashing of the freezing ocean. They pleaded desperately for help, but the lifeboats could not risk turning to save them.

Through fifteen hours of torment on the boat, the contralto Greta Williams began to sing a beautiful prayer: 'O rest in the Lord, wait patiently for me'. The survivors continued the refrain, hour after shivering hour. Eventually a pale dawn broke and deliverance came as the SS *Vera* scooped them to safety.

The horrific Victorian tragedy was done. A Board of Inquiry met in due course to dissect the evidence. The crew, it determined, had acted impeccably. 'South Western men behaved like bricks', in the words of one survivor. The disaster was pinned squarely on the captain's poor judgment, and any suggestion of ships 'racing' was swept under the carpet. Yet the sailing timetables were quietly altered so that direct competition was impossible. Then the survivors limped home, and the country mourned its dead.

To this day in Southampton there stands a memorial to Mary Ann Rogers, the stewardess who sacrificed her life for her passengers. Her image is immortalised too in stained glass in Liverpool Cathedral, the story of her mercy frozen in time, as cold and beautiful as starlight.

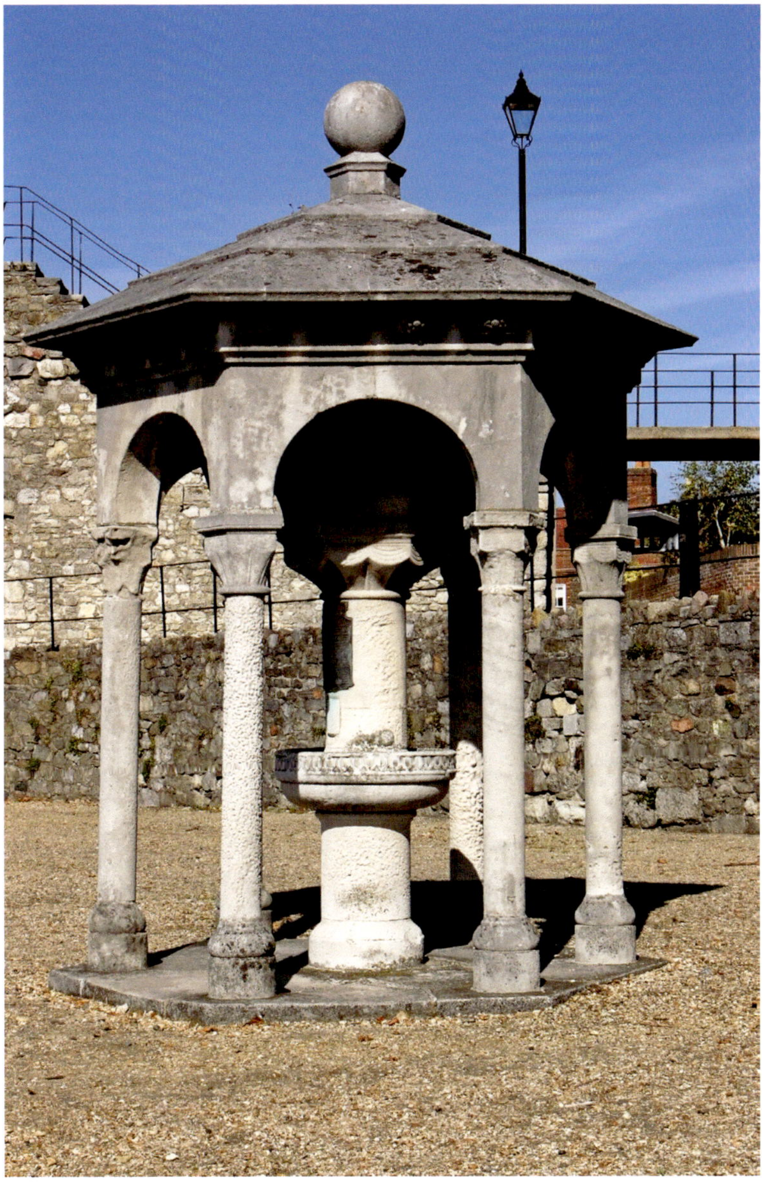

The Mary Ann Rogers Memorial in Southampton, England. (BasPhoto/ Shutterstock)

Tales of the East

In the eastern parishes of Jersey, the French coast seems tantalisingly close. On a clear day, the Cotentin peninsula stretches across the horizon. It lies just 14 miles east – hence the need for Mont Orgueil, that great defensive keep which dominates the shoreline. The reef of the Ecréhous, which belongs to St Martin's Parish, is the last remnant of the land bridge that connected Jersey to the continent until some six or seven thousand years ago.

The legend of La Planche is an ancient Jersey tale that harks back to that lost connection. Some see it as a metaphor for the great political sundering of 1204, when the Duchy of Normandy, excepting the Channel Islands, was lost to the English crown. Others catch a glimpse of a deeper folk memory, of the world where the sea was lower, when river plains stretched out to the east, before the Island was born.

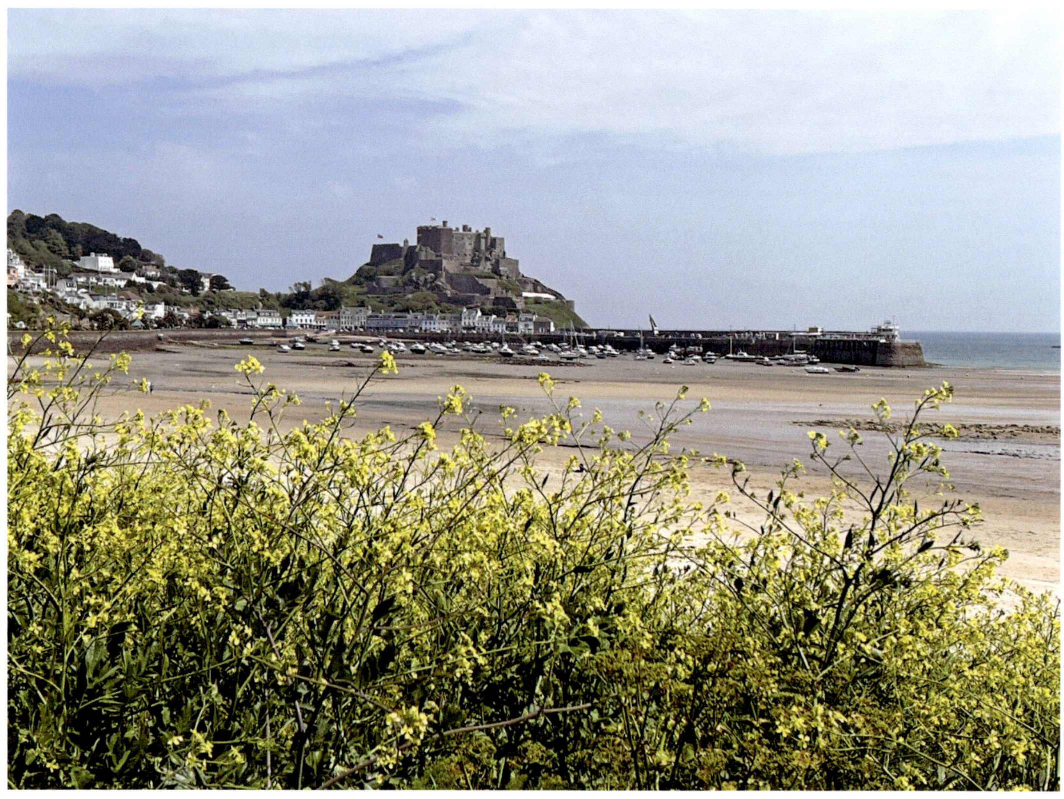

A distant view of Mont Orgueil (Gorey Castle). (Author)

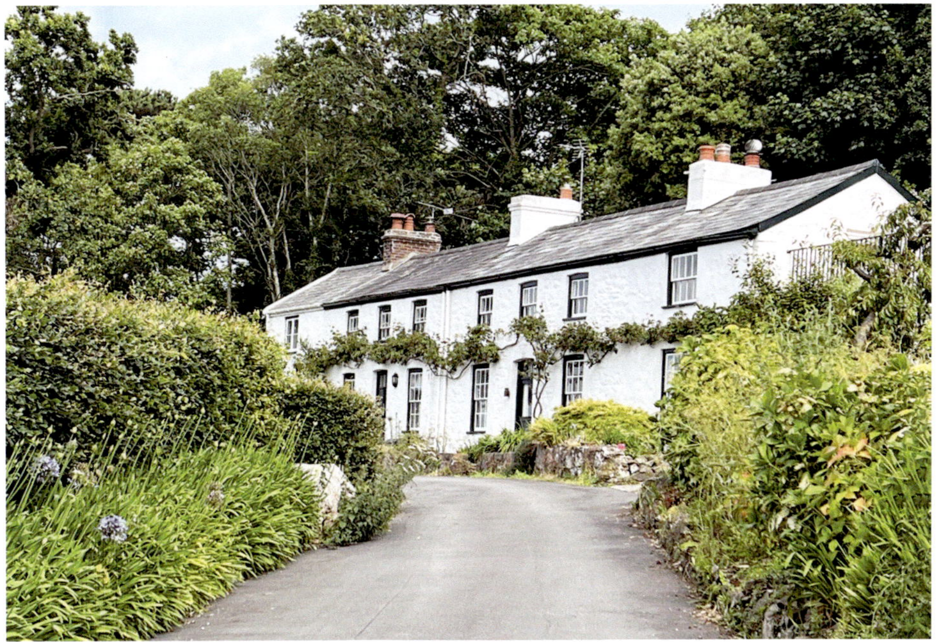

Cottages in St Martin. (Author)

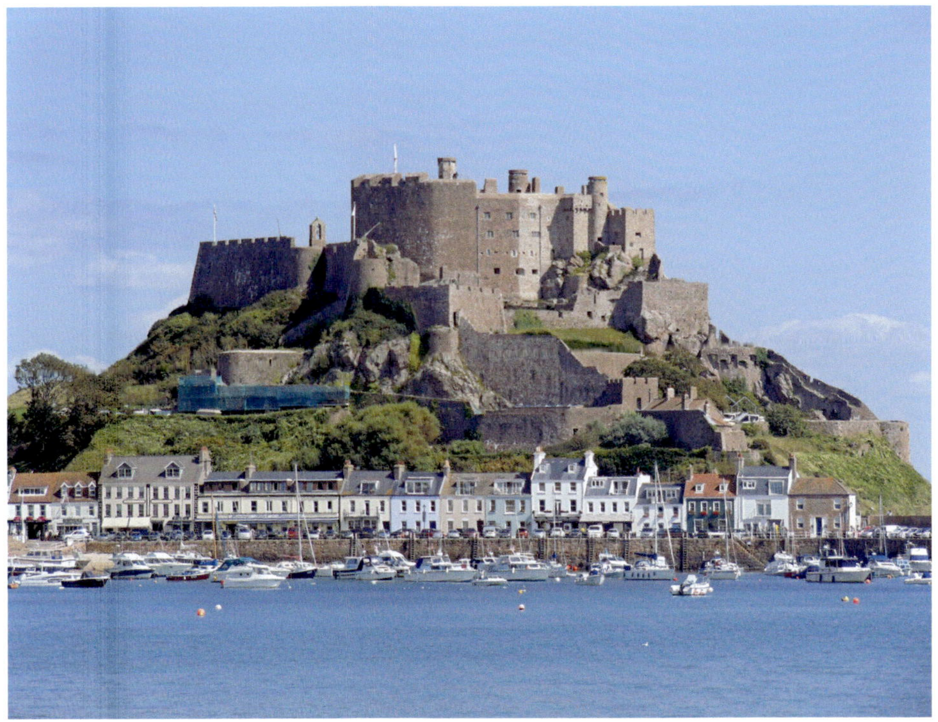

Mont Orgueil from the sea. (Author)

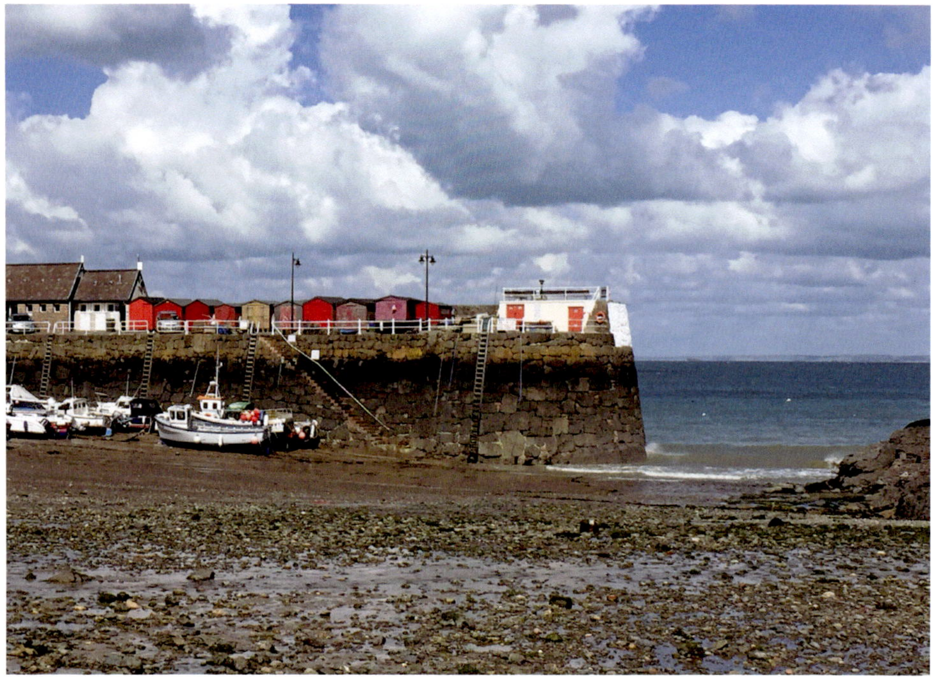

Rozel Harbour at low tide. (Author)

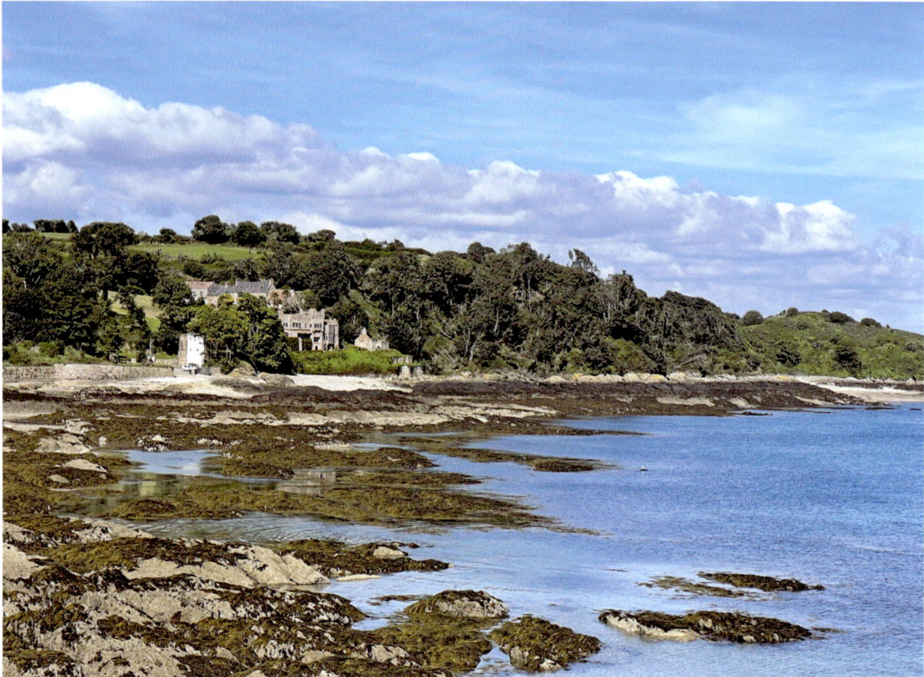

Fliquet Bay. (Author)

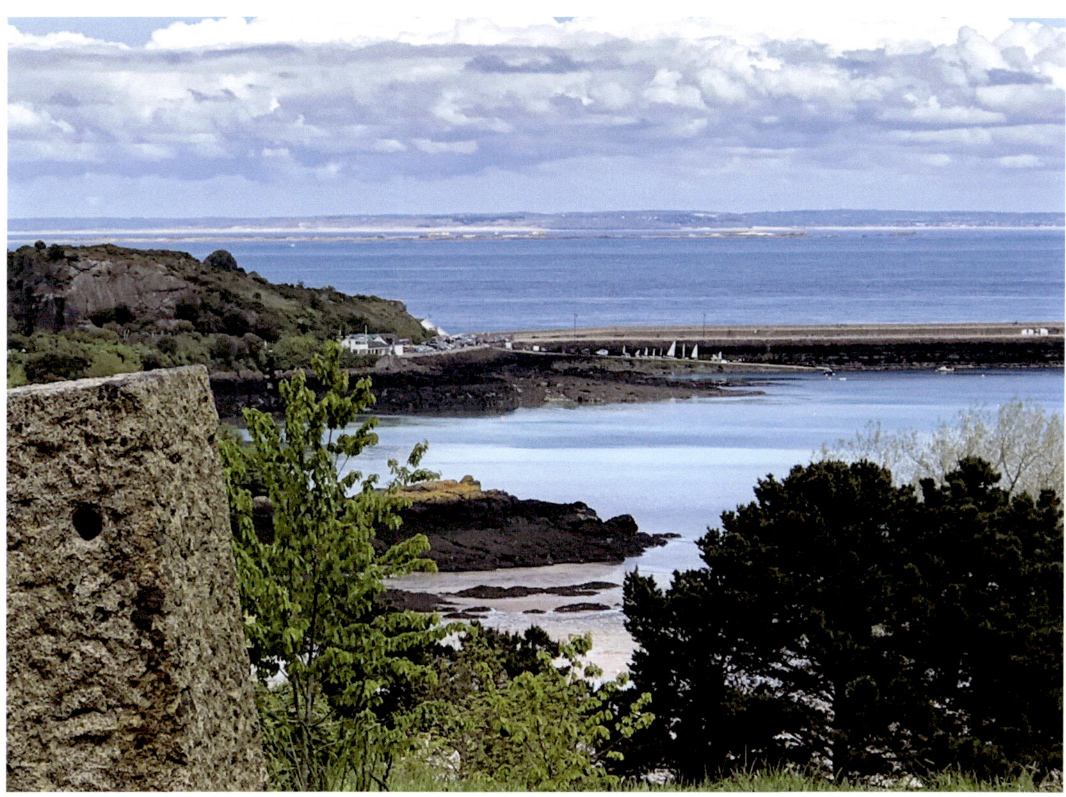

St Catherine's Breakwater. (Author)

The Lost Bridge to France

St Clement's Parish, Christmas Eve, 1355

Winter breathed ice upon Jersey. This was a season for huddling, for clinging to warmth by the embers of the fire. After the backbreaking toil of the summer, we curled up in our huts, indolent and slothful. On Christmas-eve, the goose was broiled, the turnips stewed, and we slaked our throats with pitchers of watery beer.

We were hours deep into our revelry when the storyteller arrived. He was a pitiful vagrant, a shuffling old man, the kind who lives from the alms boxes in the northern parishes. The freezing sleet must have flushed him out of the forest hole where he slept and forced him all the way down here, to our tavern in St Clement.

For an hour he stood there, as silent as a waxwork, eyes clamped shut, and he would not deign to speak. His grey beard was unkempt, and unruly hair sprouted from his ears and nostrils, a nest for lice. His clothes were feathered with snow, which gradually melted in front of the smoky orange fire. We gently mocked him, jeering at his appearance, taunting him with oaths, hoping for a reaction.

Yet he only moved when I took pity and shoved a fat mug of ale into his hand. The storyteller's eyes snapped open, and he fixed his gaze directly on me, a butterfly on a pin.

'My son, have you heard of the Drowning?'

Embarrassed and somewhat sheepish after my earlier mockery, I shook my head.

'Come closer to the fire, my son, and I will show you.' With unsettling force for a frail old man, he grabbed my shoulders and turned my head towards the belching woodfire. My eyes wept in the plume of smoke. 'What do you see?'

'Look into these flames,' he continued. 'The wood is burning and flaring, forever changing, shadows dancing and vanishing. The same is true for the hills, the coasts, the forests around you. You believe them to be fixed and ancient, but they are as new as a baby's breath.

When the world was young, Jersey was no Island. You know the salt marshes at Samarès, where the tides lap the land beneath the Seigneur's manor house? In your forefathers' day, those marshes stretched on, for mile after muddy mile, until bog and willow became solid ground, and the spires of Coutances Cathedral welcomed the weary pilgrim. We were joined to the Norman shore.

It was a treacherous, forsaken journey to cross from St Clement's Church to the other side. Men were swallowed by giant congers, choked in quicksand, or might wander till they starved, blinded by the marsh fires that blazed night and day.

Saint Lô – you have heard of him, I trust? – decided to tame this wilderness. He was born a nobleman, heir to the great castle of Briovère, yet he dedicated his fortune to the Lord's work. He was appointed Bishop of Coutances in Normandy and performed miracles, healing the sight of the blind. He desired to reach out and bless the forgotten parishes of Jersey, marooned across the vast and treacherous mire. So, Saint Lô ordered a plank to be laid down, a stout wooden bridge to provide safe passage over the marshlands. He summoned the faithful to build this great work, and had it forged sturdy and strong, with braziers marking the way.

This path was known to generations as *La Planche*. The saintly Bishop and his retinue would ride over the waters, threading their way to the Ecréhous reef, then over the violent chasm of the River Ruau, and safely across to the Grouville shore. The highway of salvation, some called it. For nigh on a hundred and fifty years, it stood proud; a roadway for the collecting of tithes, for the administration of episcopal justice, for the cure of souls.

In time, the great saint passed over to the heavenly realms, and his homestead of Briovère was renamed Saint-Lô in his honour, but his masterwork on earth remained. Yet human spite would prove its undoing.

There was a certain chapel deep in the marshes, a waystation for pilgrims to seek shelter. They say its walls were painted with the most exquisite images, of the Last Days, of the trumpet of doom and the harvesting of souls. A withered old priest lived there amongst the marsh vapours and the dreaded lights, guarding La Planche, whose strong timbers passed over his stone cell.

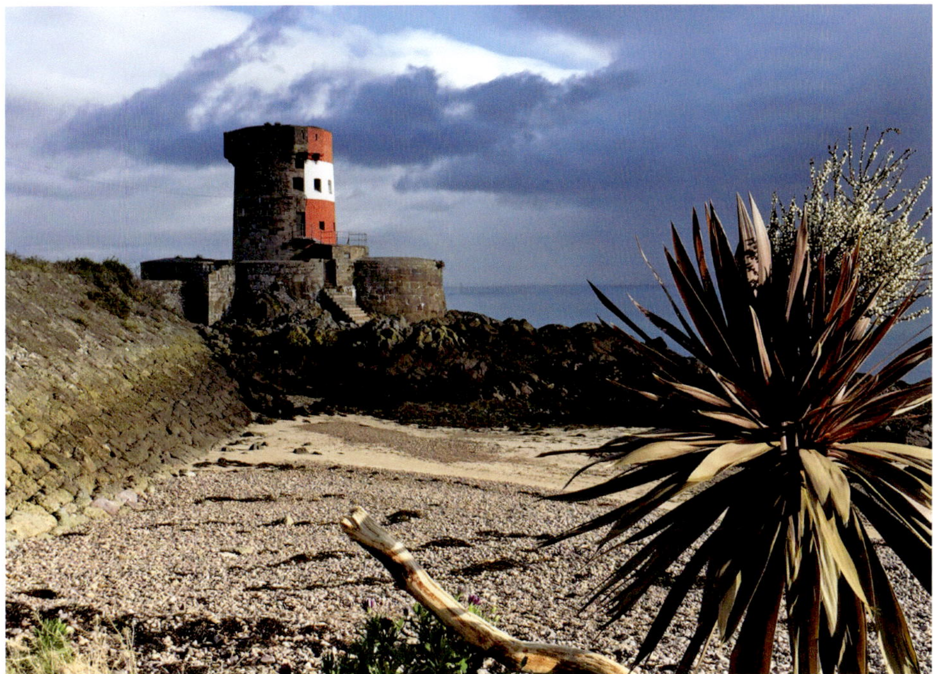

Archirondel Bay. (Author)

One freezing winter's morning, at the dawn of the eighth century of our Lord, this priest was celebrating Holy Mass alone. Picture him standing in his lonely chapel, stumbling through the introductory prayers, the Kyrie Eleison and the Gloria, those heavy Latin words ringing like iron off the stone walls of his outpost.

Above him, a shadow moved. It was a black crow, from the heart of the marsh, bilious and screeching. Its vicious cackle drowned out every one of the sacred words. In exasperation, the priest hurled stones at it, to drive it away from the rafters of his church, but it taunted him in the darkness. The feathered intruder would not yield. At last, the priest exploded in a fit of rage, launching into a tirade of hideous and vulgar profanities, uttering the most foul and vile speech. Too late he realised his terrible mistake, for in his thoughtless anger, he had besmirched the most holy ceremony of the Church.

In moments, daylight turned to blood. The weak sun was dragged down from the sky, and the marsh skies turned indigo. The ground trembled as if shivering before the wrath of the heavens, and the braziers on the bridge dimmed and died. The priest, cowering in terror, heard a great roar, as if a pride of lions was approaching his chapel. The last thing he saw was seawater bursting in from above, through the lead glass windows, with the force of an exploding dam. The very stones of his chapel were swept away by the torrent, scattered across the bed of a new-born sea.

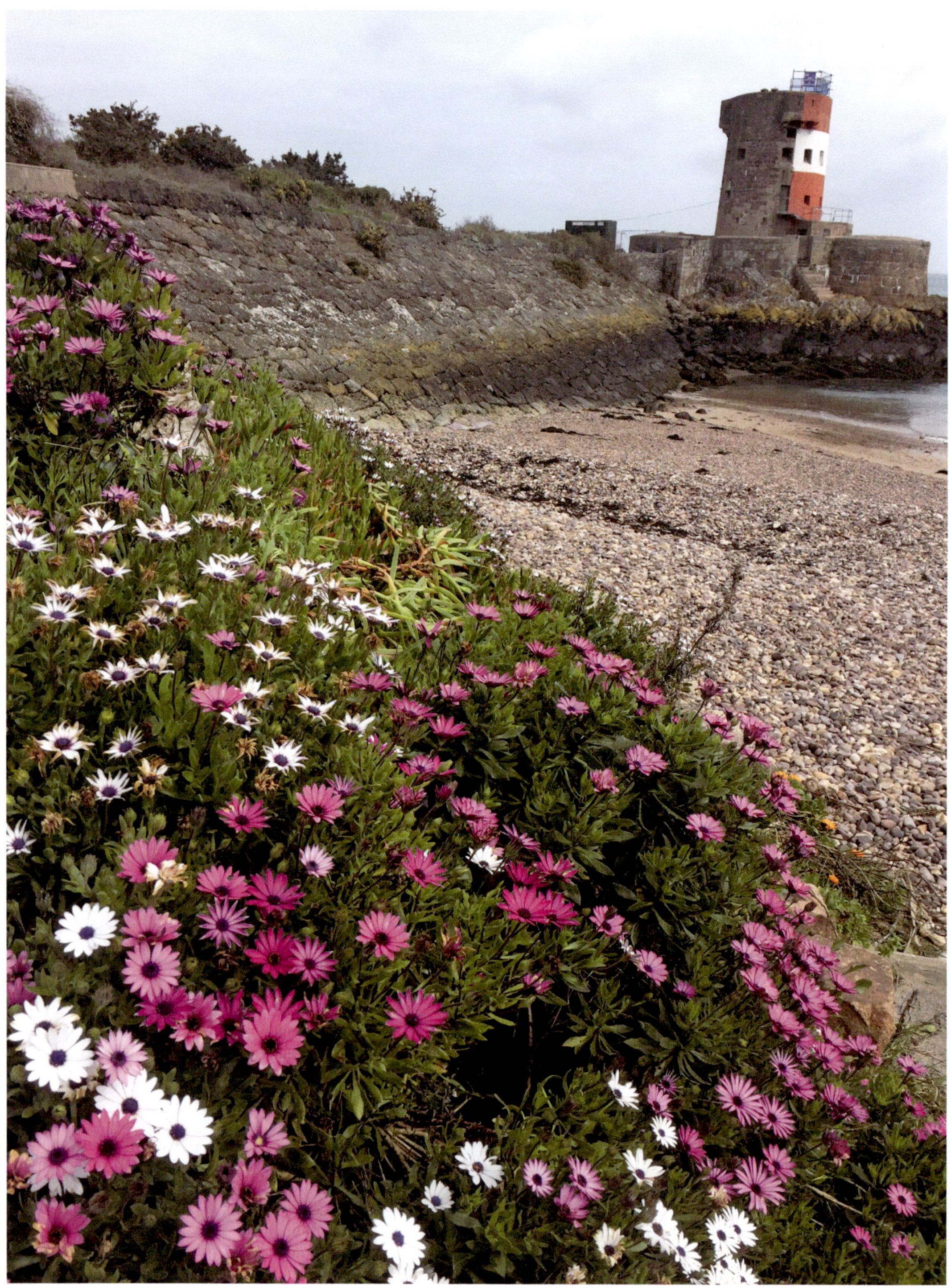

Archirondel flowers. (Author)

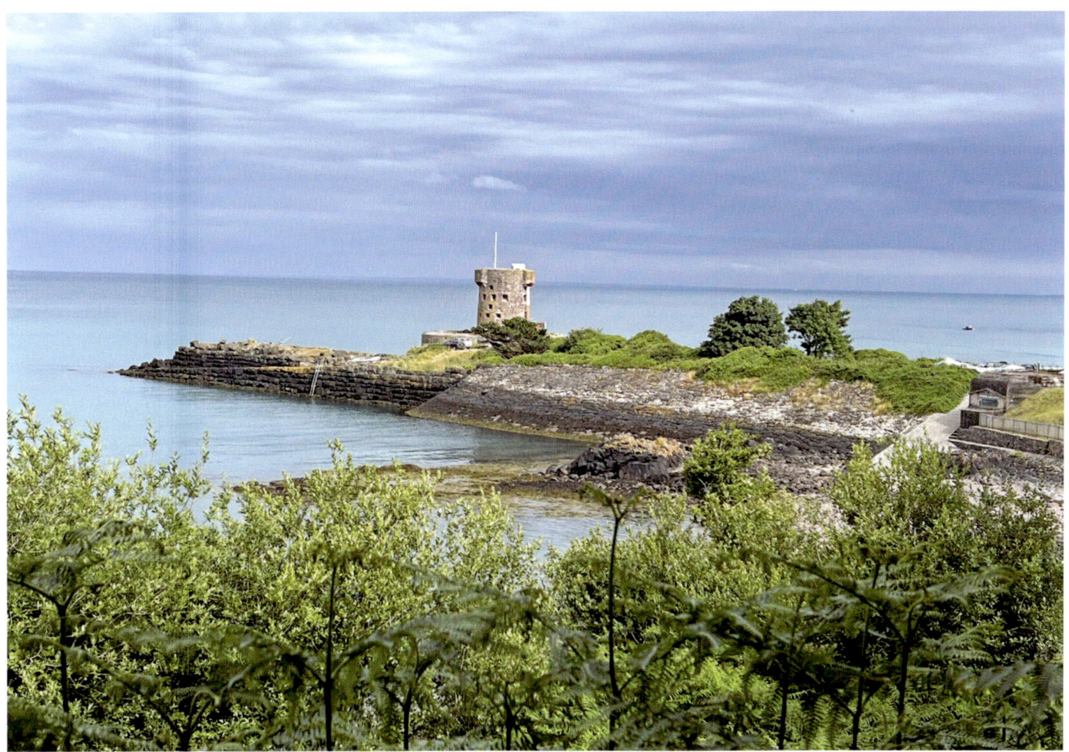

Archirondel Tower. (Author)

The cataclysm that drowned the lands in the year of 709 Anno Domini was beyond imagining. The sea flooded the great forest of Scissy and Mont St Michel, the rock in the middle of it, became an island. The long flat island to the south of Jersey slumped beneath the waves and would be known in time as the Minquiers reef. The great eastern marshes between Jersey and France were drowned and our umbilical cord with Normandy was severed. We were cut loose and set adrift, as punishment for the vanity of man.

Saint Lô's generous blessing splintered like matchwood, suddenly becoming a bridge to nowhere, a wooden plank that fell into a void. The remnants of the great plank washed up for months on our ragged shore, a forgotten raft of memories. Our forefathers burned the remnants of La Planche in great bonfires, with wailing and weeping.

Some say that the lost world has fallen from our sight but is not entirely gone. Perhaps one day these hidden lands will rise again from the deep, perhaps at the renewal of all things. But remember one lesson, my son, and this is the word of Saint James, not my own. "For every kind of beasts, and of birds, and of serpents, and of things in the sea, is tamed, and hath been tamed of mankind. But the tongue can no man tame".'

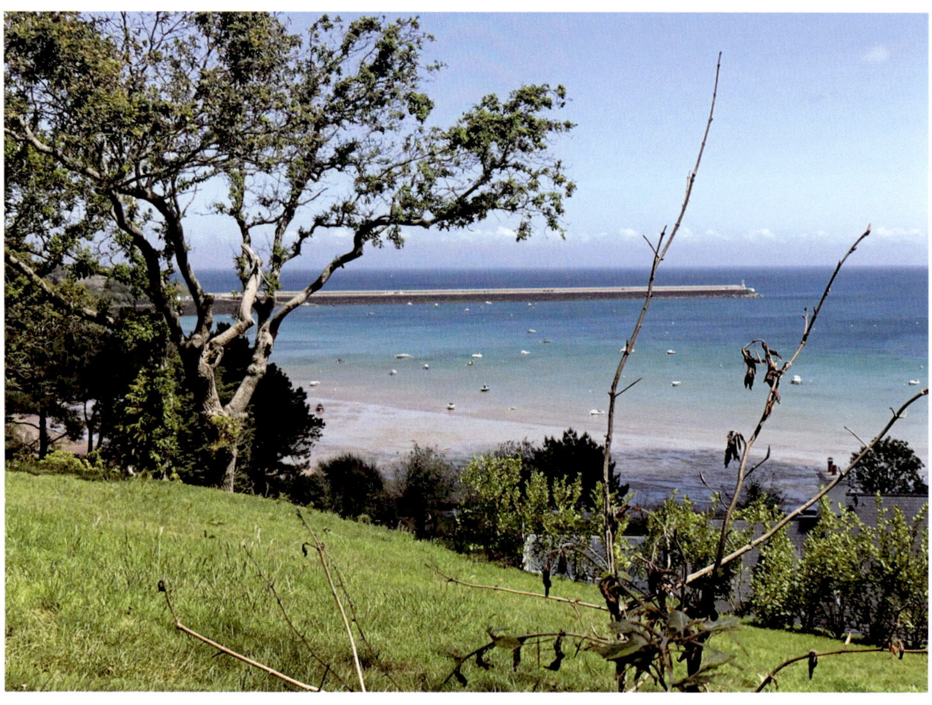

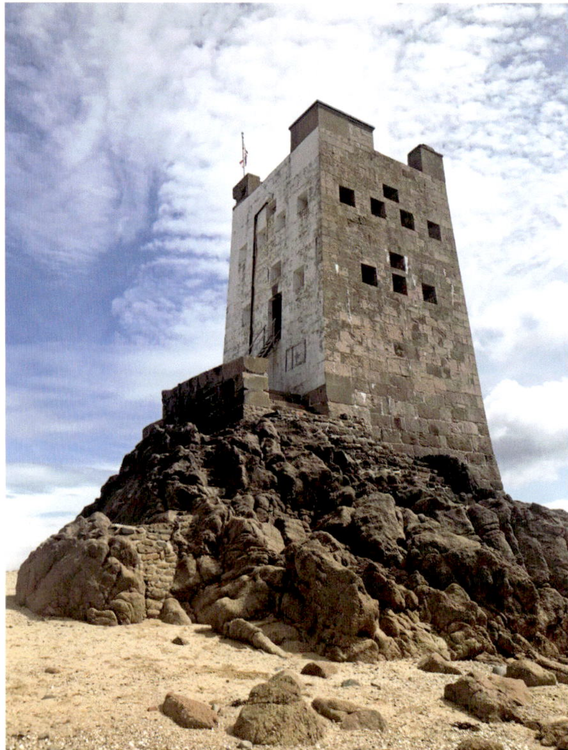

Above: St Catherine's Breakwater in St Martin. (Author)

Left: Seymour Tower in the intertidal zone. (Author)

***

In the end, they cheered the old man and threw him a handful of *sous*. The storyteller smiled, shook his clothes of soot, and set off again into the winter night. We turned back to our ale, hooting and laughing at the foolish tale of the old priest and the wooden plank. Such child's stories, mere tales for fireside chatter.

That night, I staggered home to my hut by the beach. I stared awhile at the rocks, thinking of the drowned world that once lay beyond. The sea angrily lashed the shore, the priest's curses shrieked anew in the whipping wind, and driftwood began to gather at my feet.

The Bull of St Clement

So many Jersey myths are rooted in the physical threat of the sea. Jersey experiences one of the highest tidal ranges in the world and almost doubles in size at low tide. The parish of St Clement enjoys one of the most expansive inter-tidal zones, with miles of exposed rocks and sand emerging at low water. They can quickly become fatal, as the tide surges in faster than a man can run. The medieval tale of the Bull of St Clement is inspired by the terrors of this peculiar and deceptive terrain.

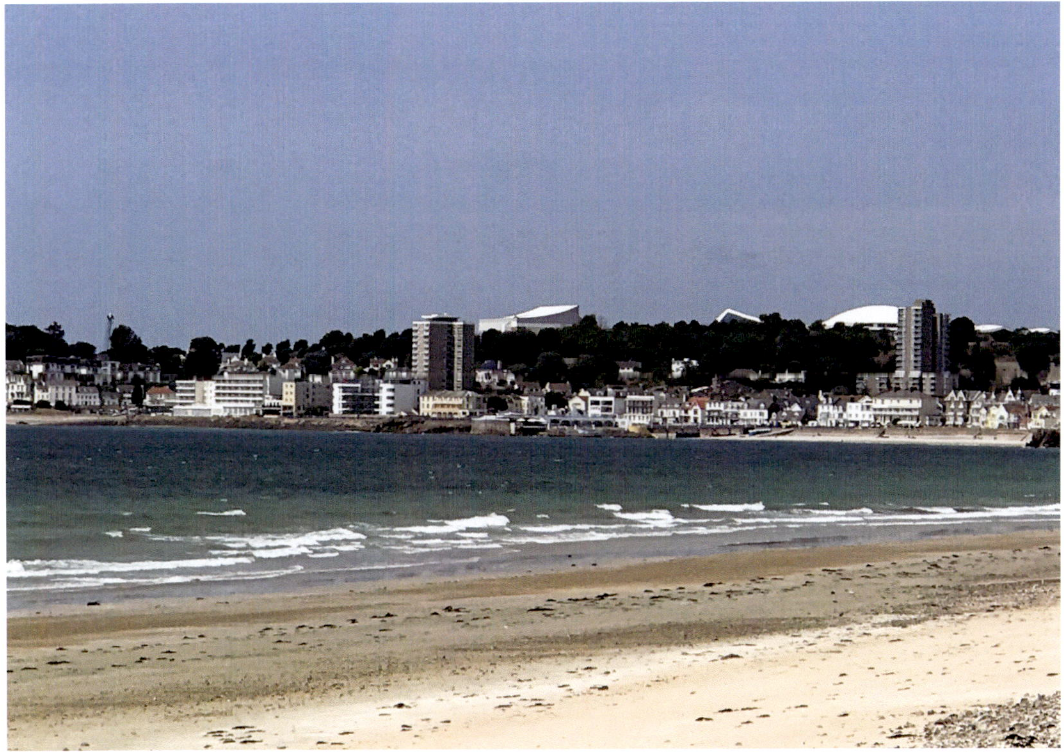

St Clement's Bay. (Author)

St Clement, Jersey, Twelfth-century AD

Jehan burst into my smithy, his tunic smeared with blood, his face raw with anger. I lifted my horseshoe out of the fire, and as its orange fire dimmed to a brittle grey, he sobbed out the tale of his tragedy.

His son Estienne had been larking on the coast, fool of a boy, led astray by his fellow herdsmen. We'd half-guessed their sport: diving for eels, daring each other to climb the needlepoint rocks, leaping from one stack to another like seabirds. They crept away from their cattle at nightfall to revel in feasts of drink and danger, as they had done on so many nights before.

Estienne came back the next morning sure enough, but without his mind. The herdsmen dragged him in, limp and bleeding, caked in mud. Jehan embraced him, warmed him by the fire, but his son seemed like an empty oyster shell that had been prised of its meat. At first, he would not eat or drink or speak. Eventually they gave him some stale beer and coaxed a few words out of him. Somehow this quick-witted, garrulous lad struggled to form each sound, as if his voice had been stolen from him. It took hours before he would even whisper the name of the terror he had seen.

We all knew how his story would end; he would live out his days as a broken man. Still, I comforted old Jehan as best I could, breaking out a cabbage loaf and a jug of watery cider to comfort him. Perhaps his son would heal in time, perhaps bread and rest would somehow salve his wounded mind.

We know the shoreline of St Clement is a vicious place; a haggard and ancient body of rock, pockmarked and bruised. It is full of dead trails and deceptive havens. Travellers perish in moments as the tide bursts in from above. This moonscape proves to be a false map, a riddle carved in rock and sand. And like any labyrinth worth its name, it boasts its minotaur.

Estienne had stared straight into its eyes.

* * *

At first light, as bloody dawn seeped over the land, I locked my smithy gate and set off to kill the beast. I was possessed by burning guilt and anger; that I, the appointed keeper of steel in this parish, should have let this terror persist.

St Clement is the patron saint of blacksmiths and metalworkers, and heaven forbid that in his parish I should cower on the higher ground, in the gentle shade of his church. My friend Jehan had seen his son's spirit broken, and I would set this travesty right. I wended my way through the salt marsh of Samarès, heading for the lurking evil of the shoreline.

I strode down to the sea alone, but I felt the shadow of Saint Clement himself walking beside me. And in my right hand, I carried one of my own creations: an anvil-beaten, freshly sharpened broadsword.

At first, we had all laughed at the story of the Bull of St Clement. The fishermen swore it was a supernatural beast, its torso swollen to the size of ten men. Its baleful breath sweeps in like December storms, they said; and its bellow explodes

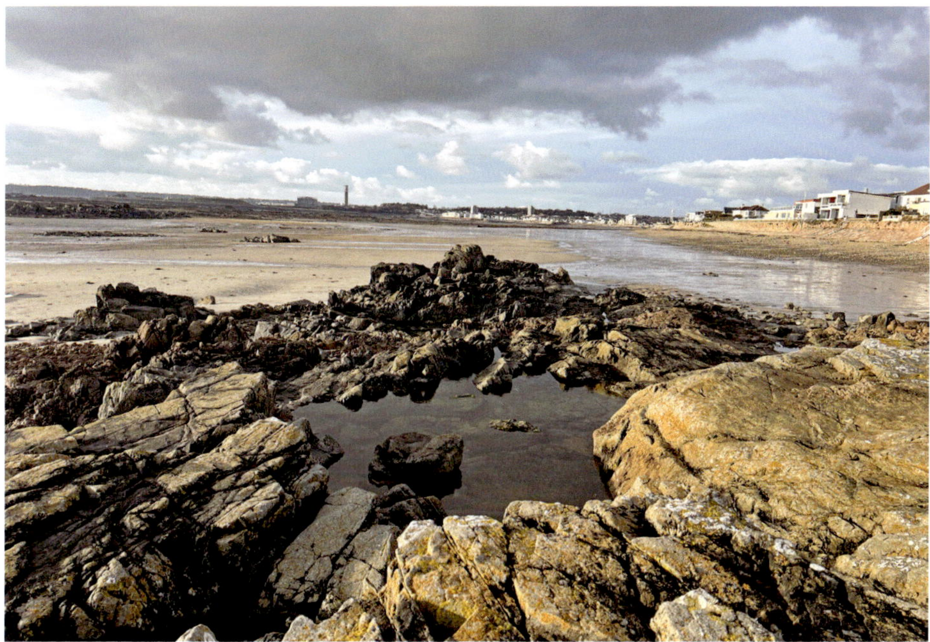

St Clement's intertidal zone. (Author)

like rolling thunder over the sands. If you happen to be thrown upon its horns, you will be gored in a moment and left on the rocks as carrion. If you gaze into its eyes, you will lose your mind.

Yes, we scoffed at first. And then the maimed men began to stagger home. Fishermen, urchins, scavenger boys, returning from the shore, cut and bleeding, most with a thousand-yard stare and a tormented mind. They heard only the roar of the Bull, raging in their heads, consuming all else. When the black night falls, the beach belongs to the Bull. It prowls freely from Rocque Berg, where they say the witches gather for their sabbats, right up to the walls of the Chapel at Notre Dame de Pas.

It is midwinter now, and a thick veil of fog shrouds the coast. So, I staked a camp by the shoreline, patiently waiting for the water to drain to quicksand and the drowned kingdom to rise up from the bay. There is no doubt; the sea owns the land here. Storms split open the shore a little further every year, claiming fresh vergées of land. Lit by a crescent moon, the crumbled desert of black rock stretched in front of me, almost to the horizon. It was time.

As the winter light waned, I sent off into the murky blackness, tracing my way through the vicious stacks of rock. I was determined to track the Bull, as I would any other beast. As I wandered deeper into this palace of stone, the coastline receded to become a black smudge on the horizon. I was soon lost in a maze of sand and reef and seaweed-encrusted pools. I heard the low rumbling of the Bull long before I saw it, and as I neared its den, I tightened my grip on the hilt of my sword.

Its bellow was rising now, a fever pitch of primal rage. I felt a creeping dread at my throat, a terrifying shiver of weakness buckle my knees. My heart was fluttering like a dove in the Samarès colomberie, but I drew my blade and scrambled on. The horrific roar grew in strength and power. I saw a shadow rustling on the rock; the stench of cow-dung, perhaps the silhouette of a goring horn. The waters were lapping at my feet as the tide hurtled towards its lowest ebb.

I thought of poor Estienne and how his wits had been crushed by this screeching valley, and so I whispered a psalm to comfort me. The twenty third, taught me on my mother's knee. 'Yea, though I walk through the valley of the shadow of death, I will fear no evil: for thou art with me; thy rod and thy staff they comfort me.'

The peaks of rock loomed like knives, and the Bull's bellow rattled through the rooms of my head. I was nearing the heart of the labyrinth. Unlike Theseus, I had no thread to carry me home. I raised my sword and stepped forward to meet my fate.

* * *

I stepped out onto a small, flat ledge surrounded by rocks on three sides. The noise was deafening. There was a torrent of seawater draining away by my feet, plunging through a great funnel in the stone.

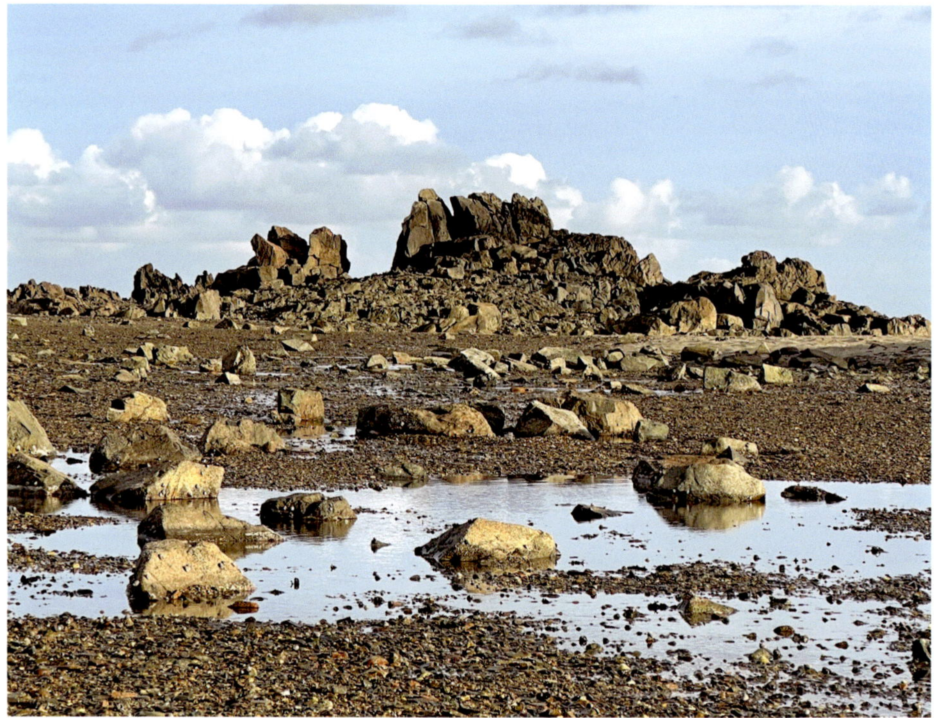

St Clement's lunar landscape. (Author)

The waterfall gurgled down and smashed out dozens of feet below, exploding into a noisy plunge pool. As the seawater hurtled back to the vanishing sea, it roared around a perfect echo chamber that created and magnified the din. Disorientated and shocked, I staggered, and in that second my blade slipped from my fingers, lost to the raging water. It scarcely mattered any more. The Bull had fled. Or rather, he had never been.

The stench around me was overwhelming; but it was not bovine dung, but a thick mantle of rotting seaweed. The eerie bellow was no beastly roar, but a clamour caused by the sheer pressure of the tide, as water plunged down the funnel of rock, echoing to high heaven off the rock walls. This terrifying valley of sound, this fear that had snared so many, was the handiwork of nature alone.

* * *

That spring we filled up the rock pipe, dragging shale and granite at low tide until the mouth of the funnel was stuffed. The savage bellow soon diminished to a child's whimper, and eventually was stilled. The priest blessed our work, and when the roaring monster was tamed, the fishermen gradually returned to the sands.

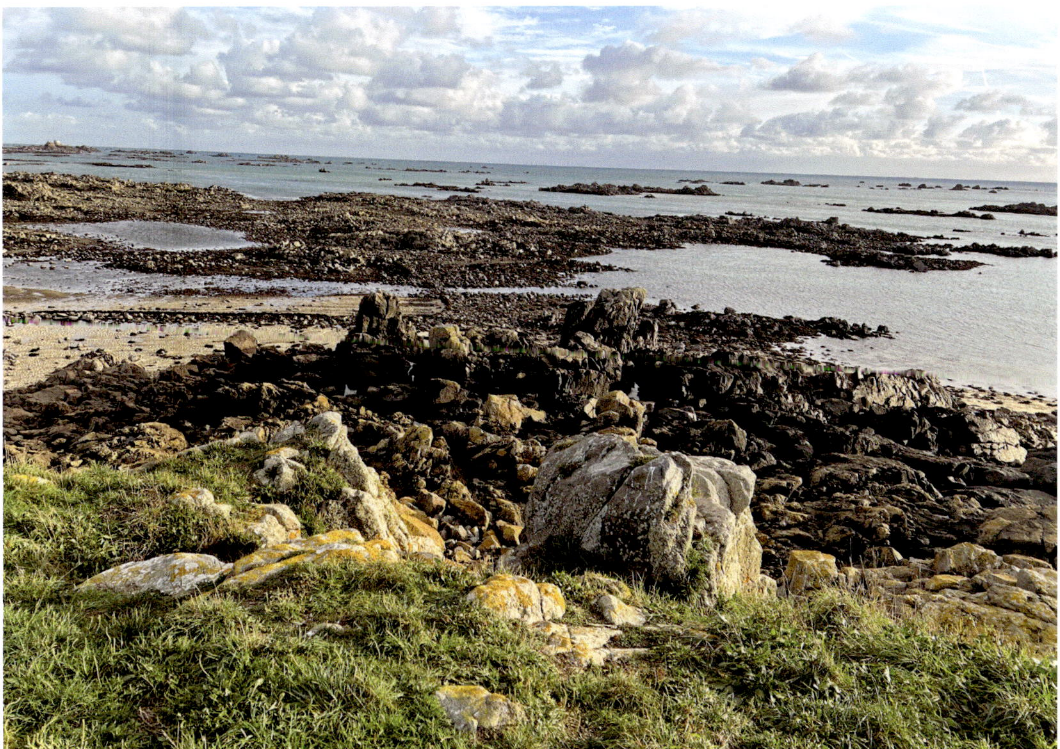

The view from Green Island in St Clement. (Author)

On the morning the work was complete, it felt as if a curse was broken in the village. When the din ceased, young Estienne sobbed and began to speak again. Minds that had been robbed of their wits were healed in moments. We gave thanks that Sunday at the parish church of St Clement for the miracle that had befallen our parish. Old Jehan and I continued our celebrations at the tavern until we slumped on the straw and the stars span around our heads. And that summer, I would forge a new and stronger blade to replace the one I had lost to the sea.

Only on the very lowest tides, on those days when it seems we marry the Norman coast anew, does the roar of the Bull return. I sit in my smithy, as the orange sparks shower around me in the night. Far away, the ancient bellow is heard again, rising from the rocks like a forgotten memory. There is something else, too; a frantic scraping, a desperate scrabbling, as if the fierce Bull is trying to smash his cage of stone and roam free again across the sands.

I sit and wait. I listen to his cries awhile, and then at last the tide turns. The Bull drowns anew beneath the rising waves, and silence floods back in towards the shore.

The Hermit King

Long ago, the Ecréhous were prominent hills above a flat river plain. When the age of the ice melted and the floodwaters rose, they became a reef stranded between Jersey and France. In medieval times, a chapel was founded there, and a great light blazed day and night to warn approaching ships off the rocks. The sea continued to lash and erode the reef, and few ever ventured to these desolate shores. Yet in the reign of Queen Victoria, one Jerseyman chose to claim it as his kingdom.

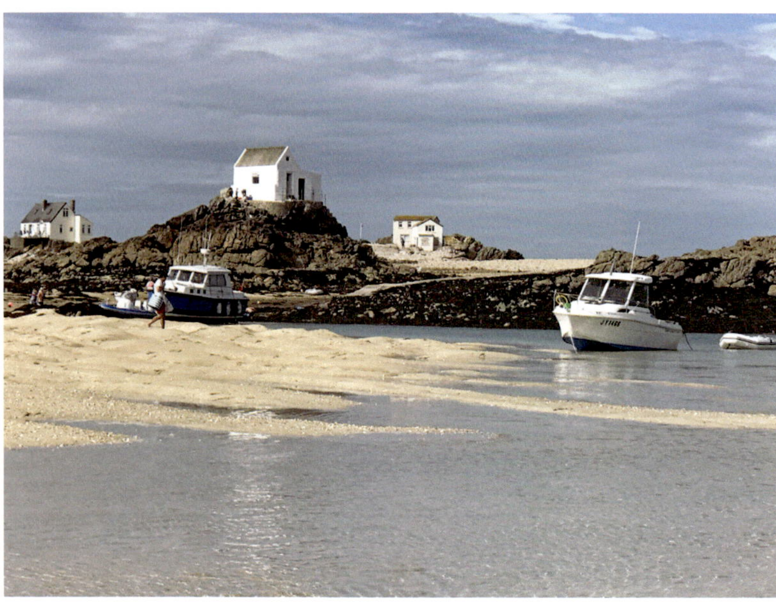

The Ecréhous.
(Author)

M. Fremine, August 1884, The Ecréhous Reef

Philippe Pinel's eyes gleamed like whetted knives. The brandy was making us all unsteady now, dragging us deeper into his story. We found ourselves fixed in his gaze like butterflies in a case.

We three Frenchmen had travelled so far, to these remote sea-hillocks, scraps of sand lodged between Jersey and Normandy. Our voyage was to pay homage to their King, to meet the old man who dwells here, many miles from the shore. We had dared to venture to the threshold of his lonely palace, and now he was holding court.

'Mark my words,' Philippe declared, 'I will die here alone. Perhaps the sea will swallow me, bursting over Blanche Ile in the dead of night, ransacking my cottage here on the shingle. Or my legs will collapse under me. On that day I will lie like a wounded seal on this reef, just as the beasts of the field lie down to die. No one will comfort me; no one will watch over me when I pass from this world.

Feel no pity for me, my friends. This is your fate, too; only you do not see it yet. Your hospitals, your towns, your priests – they are a hollow illusion. Don't be fooled. It will be the same for you in the end. Every one of us must die alone".

I almost choked on my brandy. This hermit, this half-crazed outcast, had just paraphrased Pascal, the greatest philosopher of my nation. Philippe boasted neither letters nor learning. The sea had been his only teacher, but it had taught him true.

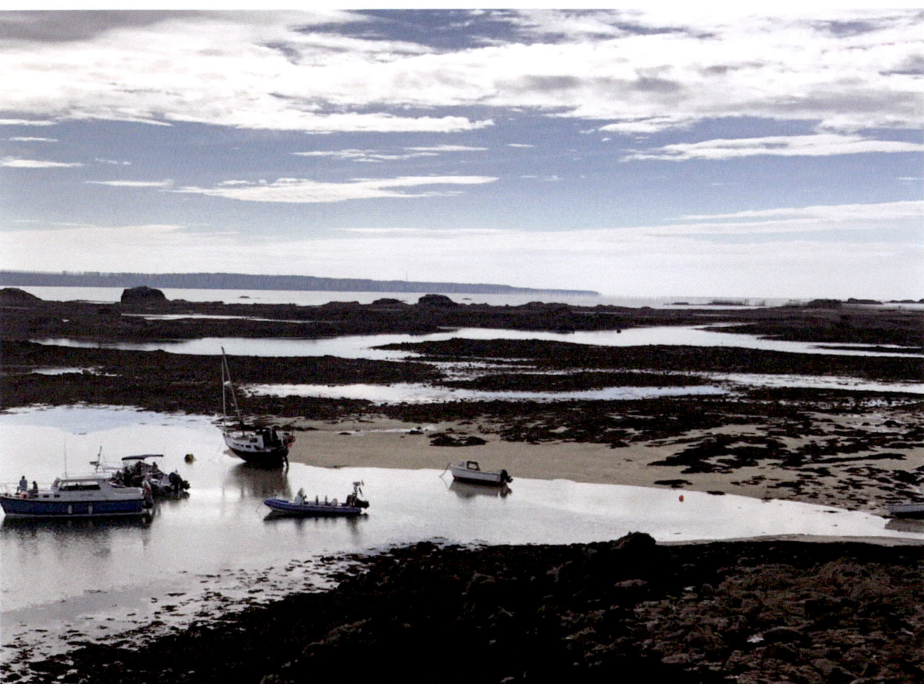

Looking back to Jersey from the Ecréhous. (Author)

With his stinging words, this wizened old man, his salt-flecked beard unkempt, his eyes staring into worlds unseen, downed another *roquille* of our liquor. The fire in the grate reared up as it devoured another pouch of seaweed, and our shadows leapt high up the walls of his stone hut, like phantoms in Plato's Cave. We had come to this hermit's hovel to learn something of him, but we had learned far more about ourselves.

We carried on drinking with Philippe for the remains of the day, until we were as slippery as wet toads. It seemed as if we supped with the reincarnation of Saint Helier himself, still imprisoned in his solitary cave. Philippe showed no interest whatsoever in our news of current events. The world beyond must have been a simple dream to him; our great nation of France a mere shadow on the wall. The name of our President, Jules Grévy, meant absolutely nothing to him; but neither I suspect would the name of Bonaparte himself.

** * **

They say the Ecréhous were once proud and mighty hills, in the days before the flood engulfed them, tearing Jersey away from its mother continent. Now only their highest summits still perch above this drowned world. In medieval times, the Priory of St Mary the Virgin stood here on these salt-lashed rocks, and the monks maintained a lamp by night and day to guide ships home. But rising floodwaters and greedy quarrying had breached the isles again and again, and now none dared to live here, in the kingdom of the sea. Save for one.

Travelling north from St Malo, we had spied the rocks at nightfall, their noses poking like seals above the waves. We moored upon Maître-Ile under a white moon, and as the sea rapidly drained away, the three of us stumbled across the lunar terrain to Blanche-Ile. Two rough stone huts, seemingly remnants from the prehistoric era, loomed dark upon the strand. One appeared to have an entrance, a wooden hatch. We knocked on this 'door', loudly and insistently, heedless of the hour.

The stars burned above us, and the night gave us no answer. We waited awhile under the indifferent moon. Then at long last, we heard a voice.

'*Quéche qu'est là?*' 'Who's there?', it boomed, in the archaic vowels of Jersey French, words plucked straight from the medieval age. 'Friends', I replied. There was only silence, so dark and deep that the night might swallow us up. Then I elaborated further: "Friends with liquor".

At once the door slid open on a groove, and a rough and hairy hand poked out of the hut, followed by a wild face, weathered in the moonlight. His eyes were luminous, his beard unkempt, but with a generous wave of the hand, he beckoned us into his sea palace.

Philippe Pinel's sanctuary was a granite hut built on the churning shingle. The carpet of his home was fine sand. He had a rough hearth and grate, but no coal; he simply burned *vraic* for warmth. The stink of his seaweed fuel was overpowering at first, but after a few minutes, one simply breathed it in and forgot. He owned a strong wooden table, but it boasted no ornaments of any sort, just a precious Bible and some well-worn liturgies.

This man lived the life of a hermit, isolated and alone. For nigh on forty years, his loyal wife Jeanne had weathered the storm here with him. Yet despairing of his drinking bouts and despotic manners, she stowed on a passing boat to Jersey and never returned. Philippe was remarkably unruffled when we enquired of her. Then a sudden smile broke over him and his eyes glinted in the dark. 'But if you wish to bring a new wife for me from the mainland, be my guest!'

We laughed awhile. Then he baked some bread for us, stewing it in a metal box wrapped tight in seaweed, as if he was preparing some kind of cabbage-loaf. For him this is a feast, a respite from his perpetual diet of fish. If he desires the rare luxury of eggs, he relies on a brood of hens nestled in a stone outhouse – the second hut we had seen. There is no freshwater here, so he must collect whatever he needs to drink in a rain-butt. In summer, he says he will often go thirsty for days.

Philippe lies down to sleep every night on a bed of stone, like a desert saint. He protested that he did, in fact, own a mattress but it was drying outside. True or not, tonight he was resting on a pungent eiderdown of raw seaweed, draped on the granite. It was a mild August night, but in the snows of winter, the chill must have cut him to the bone.

Philippe's only house companion was a thrush, who had landed long ago on the rocks. He said it was wounded and exhausted when it landed, almost ready to die. He'd nursed it to health and placed it in a willow cage hanging from the wall. It darted around, agitated at first, but even when it calmed down a little, none of us could coax it to sing.

The feast was ready. Under the beady eye of the thrush, we sat together on the sandy floor and ate. I opened the flask of cognac, and we passed it solemnly around between us. I watched Philippe drain half the bottle, and a glow creased his scaly, wizened face. Outside, the sun was rising in the east, the sky glowing over the Cotentin, the first pink fingers of dawn. Around us, the tide had turned and was beginning its creeping invasion of the reef. An old man sighed, his breath rasping with age.

Then the King of the Ecréhous began to tell us his story.

* * *

Philippe Pinel, King of the Ecréhous
The reef was empty, the shingle freshly laid, when I first set foot on La Blanche Ile. Of course, I wasn't born here, but up in St John's Parish, by the high cliffs of the north. Yet I was truly reared at sea, sailing every day with my father; you see, saltwater is in my blood. Fishing provided my livelihood and my joy, and it was the lure of conger eels that first drew me to these rocks. Baking on the reef one

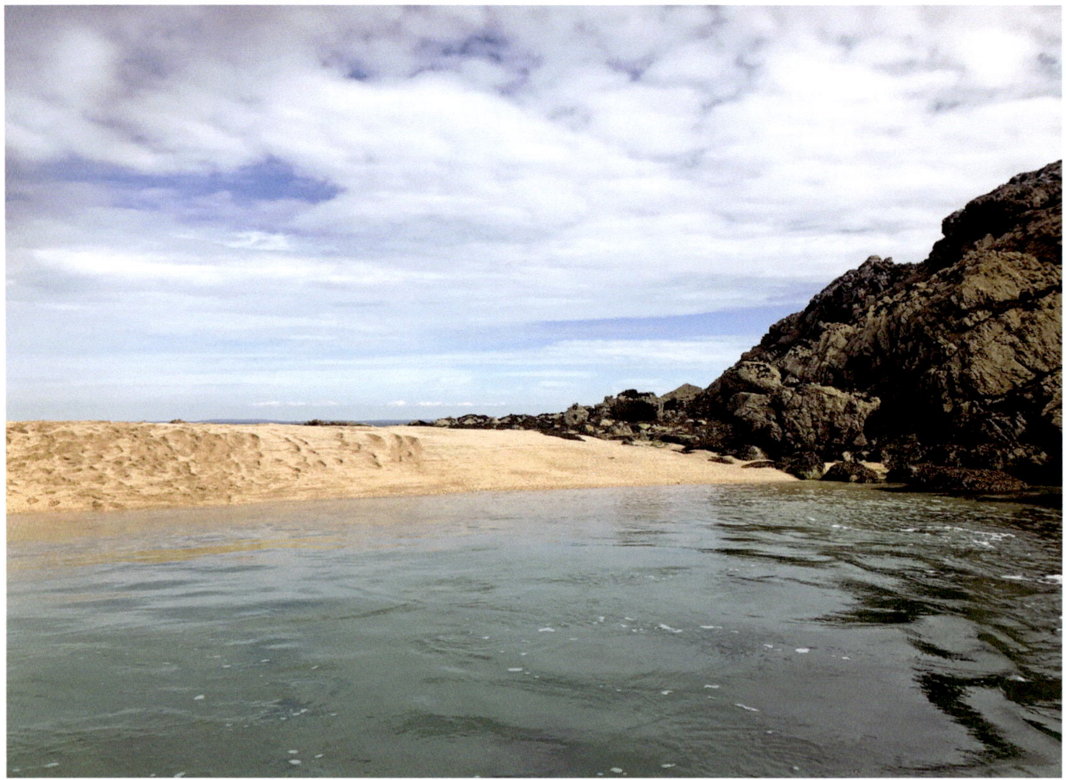

A sand bar on the Ecréhous. (Author)

morning, my line and nets in hand, staring back at the shore, I realised suddenly that I needed nothing more. Let other men keep their parishes, their ploughs and their boundary-stones. Let them squabble and toil over fields. I needed no Seigneur to bow and scrape to; no Rector to cure my soul. The sea would be my kingdom.

At first the years raced by like sunlight. The pattern of my life was plain: sunrise, high noon, sunset. I built these stone huts with my bare hands. My bones were bleached by summer heat and numbed by autumn rain. In the warmer months, the rocks were visited by tribes of sailors, holidaymakers, fishermen. In winter, when waves burst over our heads at high water, we simply clung on for our lives. In the worst storm surges, when Blanche-Ile itself was threatened, we fled to our stronghold, our shelter on the summit of La Marmoutière. We cowered behind our great stone shield and shivered for the storm to pass.

My wife Jeanne was by my side then. We squabbled like ferrets and then sulked for weeks. But here we endured, and over the years, the sea slowly started to yield its fruit. I collect *vraic* here and burn it on the rocks, like the monks of old with their lantern in the night. I can sell the embers for a king's ransom. The Jersey farmers tell me they nourish the potatoes like mother's milk.

In time, men began to speak of me; they whispered tales of this strange man who haunts the lonely rocks. Some say I am an accomplice with the travellers of the night, the smugglers who land secret cargos of wine and gunpowder and lead. I smile and let them believe whatever they want to. My fame in the Islands began to spread. Boats passed close, to catch a glimpse of me. And on a strange day in high summer, I was crowned.

The Deputy of Trinity, M. Philippe Nicole, travelled over to preside over the ceremony himself. Mr Foot, an Englishman, had brought a fine case of champagne and a generous selection of brandies. His friend, Mr Noel, helped him carry them ashore. A gang of fishermen, my vagabond brothers, had wind of the enterprise and made themselves comfortable at my hearth.

We drank for three days until we were all blotto, drunk to the point of oblivion. We sang songs, fishermen's chants, some centuries old. We sang of our Viking forbears, who travelled up the Seine and peopled Normandy, songs of victory and longing, of the sea and of the wheel of the seasons. At last, they unveiled an iron crown, specially forged for the occasion, and they placed it on my head.

On the third day, they slipped away. I was left to rule my lonely kingdom.

* * *

Let me tell you about the storm. It struck from the north, like a boxer's punch, smashing straight into the reef. Jeanne and I cowered in our stronghold, as the November rain lashed at our refuge and the damp seeped into our bones.

And then I heard the sound of a forest falling; as if a thousand trees had been felled at once, and a cacophony of screams. I feared for a moment that the Apocalypse itself had come, and the angels were busily rolling out their scrolls. I stumbled out into the night, and a tall black cliff loomed over my head. I was in the shadow of a great ship.

This was no mere fishing boat. A ship – a great, oceangoing barque – had collided directly with the reef. The rocks had already started to grind into its hull and though it stood tall as a townhouse, it was at perilous risk of breaking up on the Ecréhous. Lanterns illuminated the name on the prow – *Isabella Northcote*, of Christiana. Later I would learn it was an Atlantic trader, 200 tons in weight, hauling a cargo of timber from Montreal to London. A twist of fate, a little misbegotten navigation, had led it astray to founder on my little reef.

The storm surge pounded in; the foulest weather I'd seen in years. The ship was beached and wounded, threatening to break in two. I watched the sailors launch a small lifeboat from the deck, but as soon as it touched the surf, it was holed below the waterline. Like a child's toy, the lifeboat splintered. In moments, men were clinging to spars of wood, strewn on the waves like straw. I knew they would be dead in minutes, either punctured on the reef or numbed by cold until their hearts froze.

A fierce anger burned in me. This horror could not be permitted to happen by my own hearth and home! So, I waded straight into the bitter sea to help them, for I know the pattern of these rocks like my own skin. And other hands soon joined me, for men of Rozel had seen distress flares, and Charles Blampied, Elie Whitely and John Bouchard had already approached with a rescue boat and scooped up six men from the brine. A dozen remained aboard the stricken vessel.

Together we worked like oxen, hauling in the twelve bedraggled men, bringing them to my hut. Jeanne brewed tea for them and gave them bread; we let our seaweed fire blaze away their shivers.

A dozen men huddled round our grate, Norwegians for the most part. They knew not a word of Jèrriais nor precious little English, but the look of joy on their faces needed no translation. They had been delivered from the maw of the sea; the Ecréhous had been denied their prize. The *Isabella Northcote* was a lucky ship. Every man aboard had been saved.

We were rewarded most handsomely. Mr Charles Blampied, leader of the search party, was bestowed with a silver medal from the Royal National Lifeboat Institution. His fellow rescuers were also honoured, including yours truly. I remember the very words of the letter: 'The Committee has also decided to give £5 to Pinel and his wife as a token of its appreciation of their behaviour towards the mariners.'

What do you think I spent it all on? Stout kegs of liquor, a feast fit for a king, and a happy season of card games with the fisherfolk. The rest, I am ashamed to say, I squandered.

* * *

Philippe Pinel held his merry court on the Ecréhous for the rest of his days. In 1890, he sent a surprise gift to another reigning monarch of the day, Her Majesty Queen Victoria. It was a hand-weaved basket, in three tiers, woven entirely from his beloved *vraic*. His dried seaweed offering was filled to the brim with a generous selection of plump Jersey fish.

The Empress of India, doyenne of the British Empire and ruler of a quarter of the planet, was delighted to maintain diplomatic relations with the King of these tiny rocks. Via the auspices of General Sir Henry Ponsonby in Osborne House, and relying on Philippe's friend the Seigneur of Rozel as a trusted intermediary, a communiqué was issued. The letter was presented in person by the Lieutenant-Governor, addressed to Her Majesty's 'humble cousin' on the Ecréhous reef. She enclosed her own fine gifts: a fine blue coat, fit for a wealthy seaman, and a handsome briar pipe.

Yet no earthly monarch can rule forever. In the bitter December of 1896, the fisherman king was discovered, prostrate and sick, lying down like the beasts of the field, just as he always said he would. Despite his anguished protestations, he was whisked away to the hospital, to an unfamiliar and alien world, of people and crowds and voices. He would not tarry there long. On the seventeenth day of December, the iron crown fell from the head, and the King was gone.

* * *

It was the end of a tumultuous reign. His old friend, R. R. Lemprière, the Seigneur of Rozel, marched behind his funeral procession as it wound back to the cemetery in St John. Things had come full circle. Mourning his old friend, the Seigneur bought the fisherman's hut as a memorial, and it weathered the passing decades, as the Victorian age passed into history and the flags of strangers flew on an occupied shore. Fewer and fewer Jersey folk remembered the name of Philippe Pinel, the hermit of the rocks, and he passed into the realm of legend. Only the hut lingered on, a fragment of memory.

Winter storms would return in time, screeching down from the north. And on one catastrophic night in the 1950s, the waves consumed La Blanche Ile, wiping it from head to toe. When morning came, the stone palace was gone, the shingle was freshly laid, and the reef was empty once again.

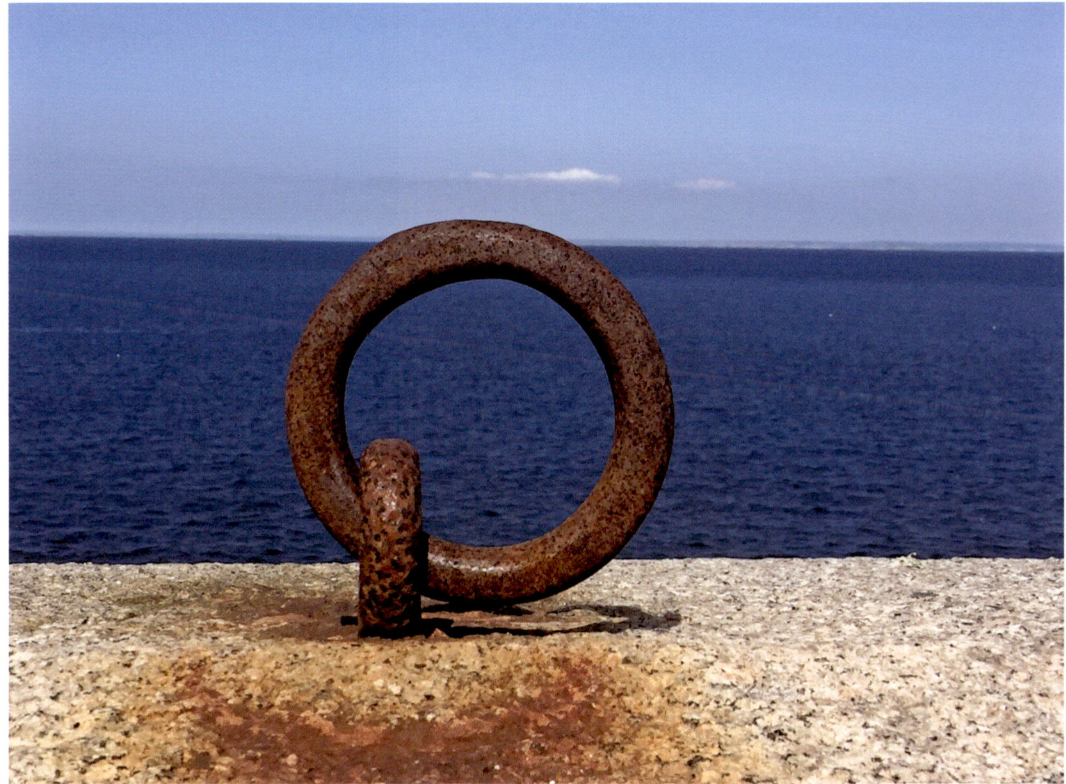

St Catherine's Breakwater – looking towards the Ecréhous. (Author)

Geoffrey's Leap

On the eastern coast road, approaching Anne Port, lies Geoffrey's Leap. The rocky outcrop is marked by a monument; but little is truly known about this tale, except the whispers of legend. The story dates from time immemorial, from an age of hearsay and rumour. It remains one of Jersey's most enduring and mysterious myths.

The Rock of Execution, St Martin's Parish, Jersey, Winter 1251
When the dawn drowned the stars, Geffray knew he was about to die. They even removed his blindfold for the final act. The hideous voices who mocked him were revealed at last: his friends, his neighbours, his brothers. The entire parish of St Martin, he realised, had come to watch him fall.

Children jostled to gain the best view of his death. A lad flung some pebbles over the cliff, foreshadowing the ordeal to come. A gaggle of milkmaids he once danced with stared at him from a distance, their whispers rustling in his ears like broken promises.

This place was St Martin's time-honoured killing ground. A boulder set high above the gentle harbour of Anne Port, it overlooked a lethal scree. The rocks below shredded any man who fell. From ancient days, criminals had been cast into the void here, and none had returned.

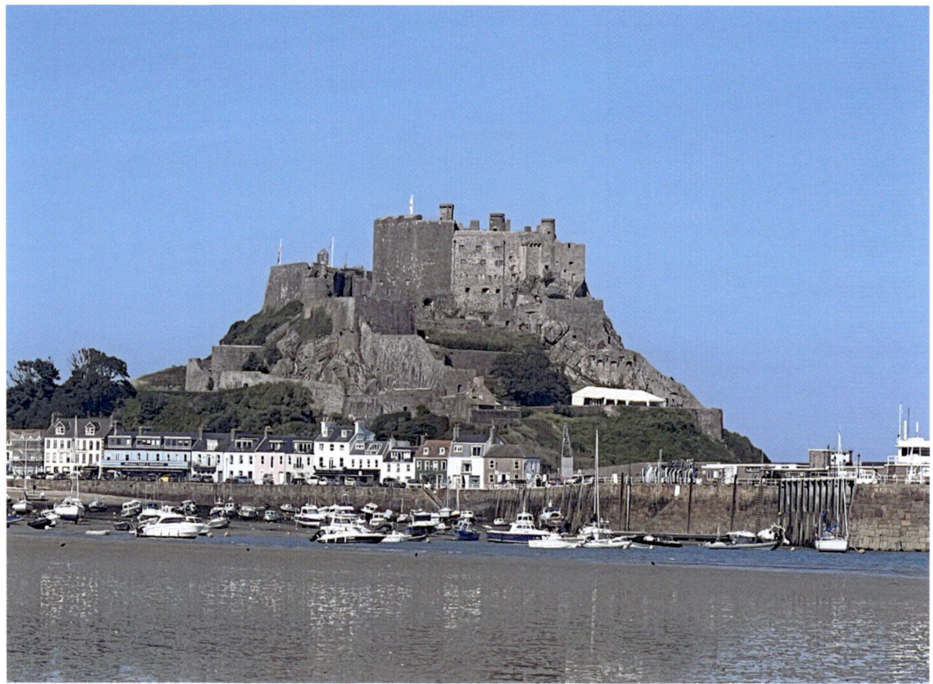

Mont Orgueil (Gorey Castle) at low tide. (Author)

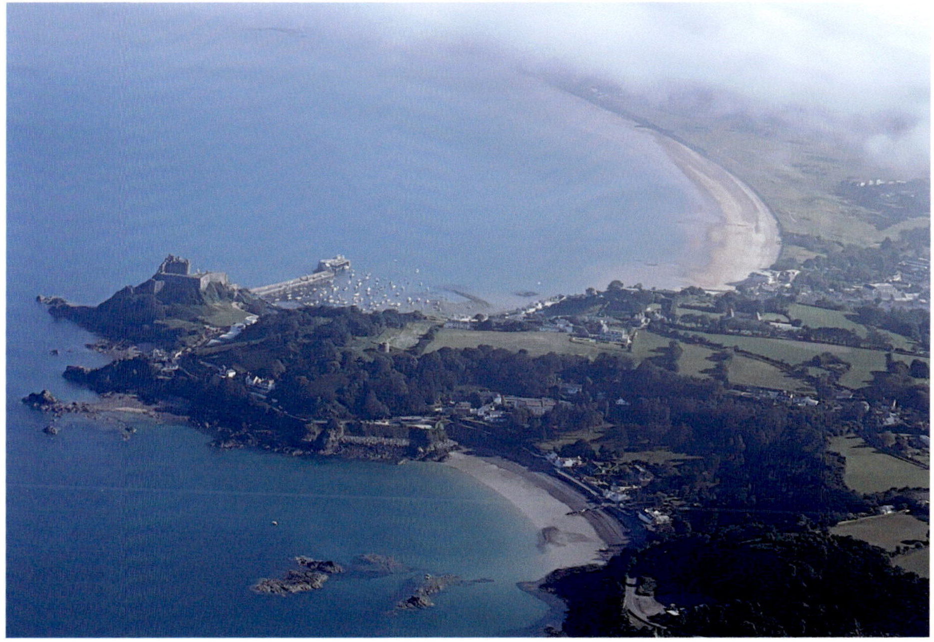

Mont Orgueil from the air. (Author)

The stragglers to the show were making their way in now; old men limping in from the fields, their backs twisted by the plough and the ravages of age. A squad of militia from the castle strutted round the headland, bearing halberds. Spinsters and seamstresses, farm boys and grooms; all had come to see him die. Even the fishermen had come to gawp, watching from their boats out in the bay.

Silence fell like frost. The Rector of St Martin fidgeted in his cassock, sweating and ruddy despite the chill of the morning. Behind him, the Jurat loomed, as unyielding as granite, a scroll from the Bailiff clasped tight in his hands. Some said Geffray's crime was so flagrant, so shocking, that the Warden of the Isles himself had intervened to pass sentence on the malefactor.

The red sun began to rise, a bloodstain curdling the eastern skies. It burst up over the horizon of Normandy, bleeding into the drowned valleys. As the light grew, Geffray noticed a raven-haired lady had joined the throng. The crowd murmured. All eyes were drawn to her fierce beauty, for she strolled with a magnetic grace. It was Ysole of Rozel herself, the wronged woman, draped in the black robes of mourning.

Geffray had been her plaything, her daytime companion. Hers was an open bed, and of course he knew all about her husband, the ploughman Renaud. The two men drank deep of the same befuddling wine. Yet Geffray knew she was besotted with Renaud above all, for she would always breathe his name. Renaud became the shackle that dragged at his feet, the unseen mocker who taunted him, even in his dreams.

And one night, in the darkness of a tavern, the men would meet. Jealousy raged like wildfire. Words flew, then fists, and Geffray felt the racing panic of a chokehold at his neck. He fumbled for his hunting knife, and the night burst open like a bloody heart. Renaud died beneath him in the straw, his dark blood pooling around his strong ploughman's arms.

Geffray was now a killer; he could expect no mercy. He was cast down into the punishment pit at Gorey Castle. There he was abandoned without food or water, his mouth bloated by thirst. On the third day, he stammered out his confession.

Only then did they bring him a pitcher of watery ale, along with a black robe, the garment of the condemned. In the darkness before dawn, Geffray knew where he would soon be bound. Mont Orgueil, he realised, was an apt name, for it was pride that had brought him to this place. Before first light, a tumbril bearing the prisoner rattled out of the castle gates.

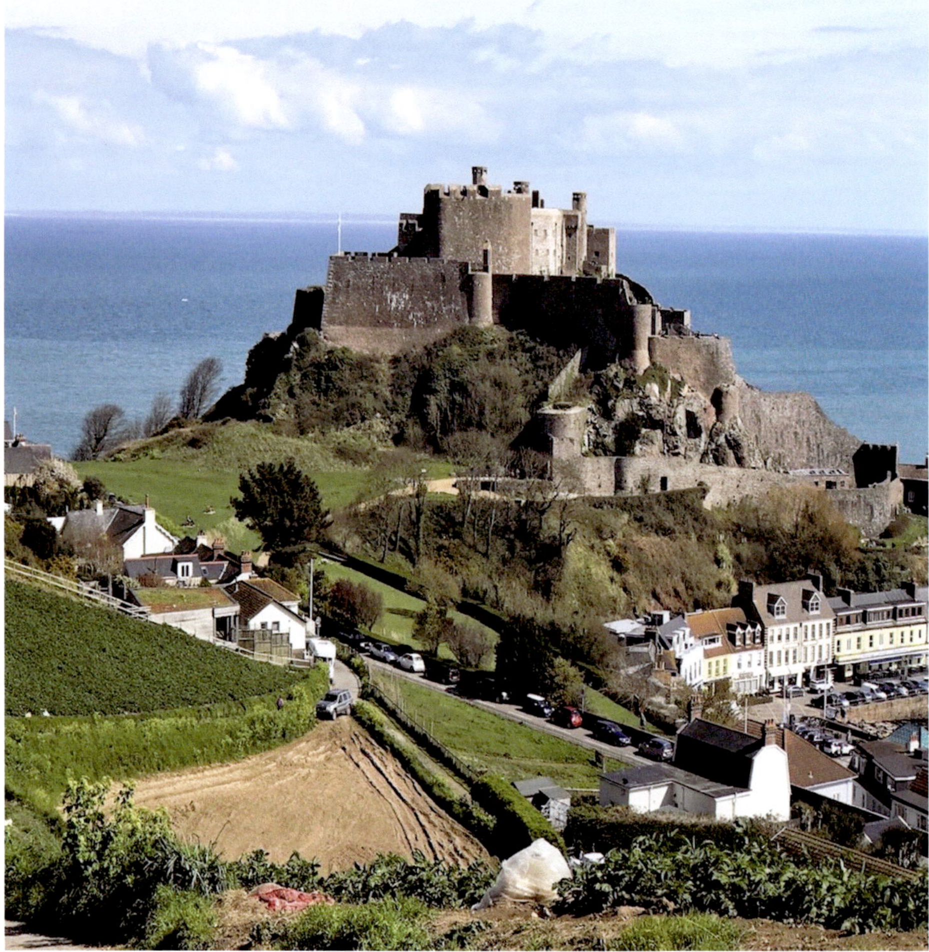

Mont Orgueil (Gorey Castle) from the land. (Author)

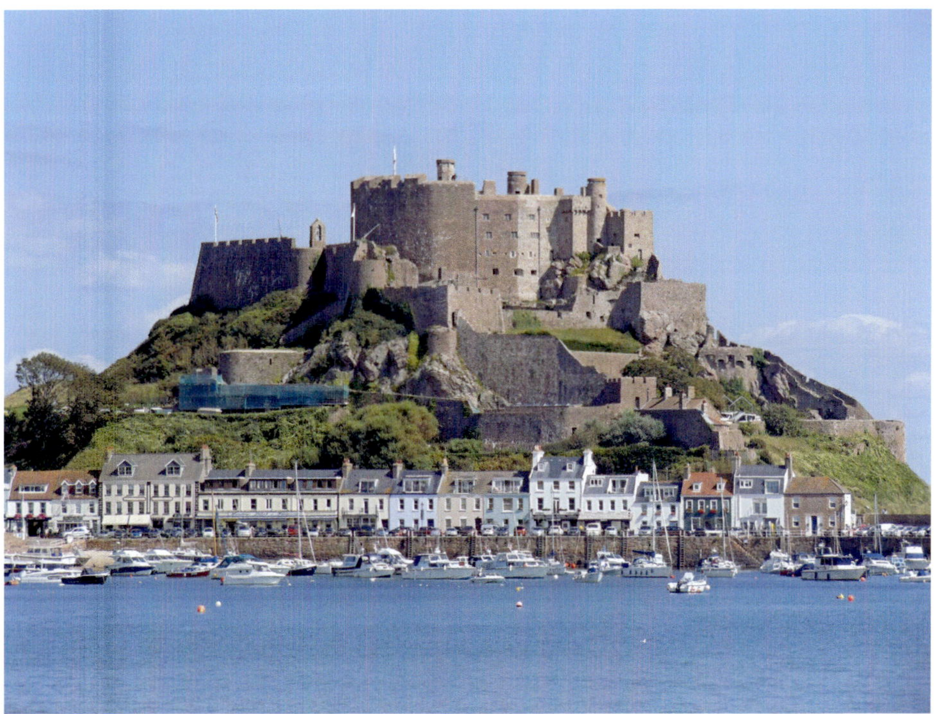

Mont Orgueil from the sea. (Author)

* * *

The sun rose, and the time to die had come. Geffray refused to acknowledge the presence of his lover, to give her the satisfaction of his tragedy. He stared only at the fat Rector, who muttered words of cold, impenetrable Latin. Seagulls screeched over the rocks, and somewhere, far off, a baby cried.

Then Geffray stood on the great stone of punishment, the place his mother had once shown him as a little boy, spoken of with a hushed dread. This rock was the door from this world to whatever lay beyond.

And he barely felt the brutal shove to his lower back, the stumble into space, and the horizon swallowing him up. The mocking of the crowd faded as if in a dream. He saw a blaze of red, felt the sea-air screeching in his ears, and the giant sun burning the sea-mist. He plunged like a stone.

Then he landed, knee-deep, in a tiny crescent of soft and yielding sand. The impact stung for a moment, but he felt no pain. A mere foot away on each side lurked a pair of massive, bone-shattering boulders. It was a sheer miracle; he felt like a baby thrust out new into the world, landing on a feather-down rug. He had cheated death, and his heart roared.

A smile slowly broke over him. Lazarus had returned from the grave. The men on the ledge had witnessed this resurrection and watched slack-jawed in astonishment. Then Geffray vaulted up the shallow slope in the mid-bay and strode back in strength and majesty to greet them all.

The crowd retreated before him, dumbstruck. Even the Rector crossed himself as Geffray crawled up from the land of the dead. A shiver of awe rippled across the throng. This time, Ysole was waiting for him. Their eyes met; hers flashed with the colour of cornflower. Her love shone raw and true, as keen as a hunter's blade.

Now the world was Geffray's, and everything was whole again. A surge of bravado, of wild exuberance, gripped him. He looked beyond the Jurat and Rector and addressed the court of his peers. 'God has judged me in this trial, and behold, I am an innocent man! I will leap once again now, to show that your laws can never bind me in chains. I am a free man of Jersey, and this is the testament of my freedom.'

The Jurat blustered, purple and indignant. But no one dared touch the resurrected man or lay hands on him again. Buoyed by the singing of his blood, Geffray stepped back on to the rock in triumph, as a free man. The waves, the people, the cliff-face seemed to be cut now from the same cloth around him, woven together in a single tapestry.

A great cheer erupted from the crowd at last, to carry him up and over, a guttural, primeval roar of acclaim. For a precious moment, Geffray savoured it all: the red dawn breaking over Jersey, the adoration of the crowd, and the tides racing in below.

Then he leapt into the rising sun.

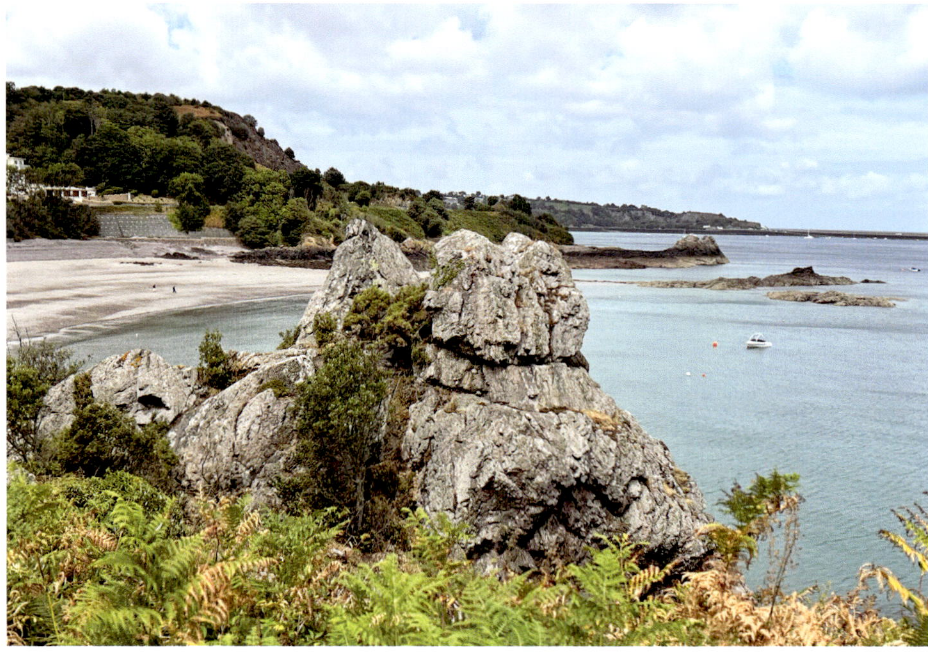

Geoffrey's Leap. (Author)

Postscript

'Man Bieau P'tit Jèrri' ('My Beautiful Jersey') is Jersey's official anthem. It was written by the Englishman Lindsay Lennox (d. 1906). This is the first verse, written in the Island's ancient language of Jèrriais, with a translation below in English.

Y'a un coin d'tèrre qué j'aime, qué j'n'oubliéthai janmais -
Dans mes pensées tréjous preunmyi -
Car jé n'vai rein à compather à ses bieautés
Dans touos mes viages à l'êtrangi.
Jèrri, man paradis, pus belle taque souos l'solé -
Qué j'aime la paix dé chu Jèrri!
L'amour lé veurt, j'ai si envie dé m'en r'aller
Èrvaie man chièr pétit pays.

There's a corner of earth that I love, that I will never forget –
Almost foremost in my thoughts -
For I see nothing to compare with its beauty
In all my travels abroad.
Jersey, my paradise, most beautiful spot under the sun –
How I love the peace of this Jersey!
Love wishes it so, I have a longing to go back
To see my dear little country again.

Translation courtesy of the Jèrriais Teaching Service.

Acknowledgements

In the years after the Occupation, many of Jersey's ancient maritime legends were painstakingly collated by Philip Ahier (1887–1975). His three volumes of *Jersey Sea Stories*, lent to me by my father-in-law Graham, inspired me to start my own exploration of Jersey's folklore.

Above all, thanks are due to Katie, Isabella, Jemima, Ian, Vicki, Graham and Jean.

About the Author

Paul Darroch was born in England and is now an established local history writer in Jersey. His publications include the books *Jersey: The Hidden Histories* and *Jersey: Secrets of the Sea*. He is also a regular history writer and podcaster at The History Islands. Paul is a former Centenary Scholar in Modern History at St Hugh's College, Oxford, and a winner of the Shell Economist International Writing Prize.